D0960831

The Lives
of Pearl Buck

A Tale of China and America

Women of America
Milton Meltzer, EDITOR

The Lives
of Pearl Buck

A Tale of China
and America

by Irvin Block

Illustrated with photographs
THOMAS Y. CROWELL COMPANY   NEW YORK

Designed by Angela Foote

Manufactured in the United States of America

921
B855b/

ISBN 0–690–00165–7

Library of Congress Cataloging in Publication Data

Block, Irvin.   75 - 104
    The lives of Pearl Buck.

        (Women of America)
        Bibliography: p.
        1. Buck, Pearl (Sydenstricker) 1892–1973.
    I. Title.
    PS3503.U198Z6   813'.5'2 [B]   73–8891
    ISBN 0–690–00165–7

1   2   3   4   5   6   7   8   9   10

ACKNOWLEDGMENTS

Where biographical facts or direct quotations used in this book are derived from individuals, magazines, or newspapers, the source is generally acknowledged together with the material. Other biographical data and direct quotations, including all conversations, come from Pearl S. Buck herself and from her books *My Several Worlds, A Bridge for Passing, The Child Who Never Grew, Fighting Angel, The Exile, What America Means to Me, American Unity and Asia, Of Men and Women,* and *The Chinese Novel,* all published by the John Day Company. *Friend to Friend* (John Day), which she wrote with Carlos P. Romulo, and *For Spacious Skies* (John Day), which she wrote with Theodore F. Harris, furnished material. Mr. Harris' biography *Pearl S. Buck* (John Day), in the preparation of which she participated, provided valuable insights, as did the biography *Exile's Daughter* by Cornelia Spencer, published by Coward-McCann. *Pearl S. Buck,* by Paul A. Doyle (Twayne Publishers), suggested some background and additional references. Elizabeth Riley vividly described Pearl Buck's debut into the New York literary scene.

In a nonfiction book one is not supposed to acknowledge fiction. But the link between life and art is especially important to emphasize in dealing with so total a writer as Pearl Buck. In seeking the sources of this, her novels, her major work in the world, are of special importance, providing a geography of her intelligence and a biography of her spirit. Their help must be acknowledged and accounted for even in this book, which contains no fiction at all.

To my family

*For "the moments of happiness are
in small things,
if you are in tune to them."*

Contents

The Lives
of Pearl Buck

*A Tale of China
and America*

One

❧

They Called Her Comfort

Caroline Sydenstricker named her baby Pearl Comfort on that day in late June 1892. Pearl, because "you were fair when you were born. Your hair was gold, your skin was white—yes, actually you had pink cheeks and a rosy mouth and the bluest eyes. You looked like a little pearl." Comfort, because this baby eased a deep hurt. Symbols of the hurt lay in a carved sandalwood jewelry box in the chest at the foot of the bed: a bracelet of delicate blue glass and a tiny thimble that had belonged to Edith, dead at four years; a little padlocked silver chain once worn around the chubby wrist of Maude, dead at six months; a lock of soft dark hair from the head of Arthur, dead at eighteen months.

The three lost children lay under little mounds of earth in China halfway round the world, and there Caroline would soon return bringing a snip of an American rosebush to plant over their graves. But she would also bring back with her this curious little girl, the only one of her children to be born in America, in her beloved West Virginia.

Edwin, twelve years old, came to watch his new sister awhile but then left for more important activities in the barn and fields. Absalom Sydenstricker, all knees and elbows and restless hands, long finger holding the place in his prayer book, came to tower over the bed and shyly ask his wife how she felt but hardly hear the answer, for his thoughts were already fastened on the return to China, made closer now by the end of this pregnancy that had kept him from his missionary work. It was from him that the baby had her cool blue eyes, but whereas even now the baby's eyes saw and recorded, Absalom's had a blind way of seeing not what was in front of them but that which was either far beyond or locked inside himself.

Then others came. The delicate, erect old man with the mane of snow-white hair was Caroline's father, Hermanus. The strong and quiet-spoken man with the sturdy footstep was her brother Cornelius, flanked by his chattering black-haired wife. All these faces and presences drifted about the child's first months of life and were perceived in flashes of wakefulness. But of course the face that meant the most was that of Caroline, her skin the color of dark cream, with dark brown hair and warm brown eyes bespeaking her French ancestry. And with that face came the most wonderful sounds, for Caroline laughed easily, loved to sing, and played the violin and organ. With the sounds came the deep sweet odors of a strong body. And the infant fastened to that body and was cheerful.

They left for China shortly afterward. There another face and another body, much darker brown, warm, and fragrant of earth, became important. That other was Wang Amah, the family servant, who waited on the wharf at Shanghai. The woman gathered the baby into her arms, shouted for happiness at this new life to care for, wept in sorrow for those who had gone, crooned "the curliest of Chinese tunes" into Pearl's pink ear, and instantly then the four-month-old child belonged half to China. The patient, round brown potato of a face seemed as right and good over her as Caroline's.

They stayed only a day at Shanghai, long enough for Caroline to plant her white rose over the little graves, and then the family took a steamboat up the Yangtze River to the Grand Canal, where they transferred to a junk that spread its bamboo-ribbed sails and, leaning creakily on the wind, took them the rest of the way to the house at Tsingkiangpu.

There the infant's world was the house and the courtyard, hemmed by a gray brick wall where Caroline's beloved roses grew. If Pearl lay on the earth, she could see through the six inches that separated the gate from the ground. The outside world was a parade of legs—bare brown feet and legs with ropy muscles, feet in straw sandals, little feet in velvet slippers —and if she put her eye close to the crack, she could see flowing robes at knee-length, all passing by unendingly.

And there was Caroline moving through the courtyard with her garden shears, stopping to romp with her children. Or Caroline could be seen through the window of the gatehouse, where she held her clinic for mothers and babies and taught reading classes. And music—Caroline teaching Edwin to play the violin, Caroline at the little organ sent her by her brother Cornelius, her gold-flecked eyes sparkling as she sang and taught Edwin to sing, too, while Pearl listened and absorbed the sound of it and grew on it as if it were food.

Always there was Wang Amah, a storehouse of Chinese rhymes and tunes, soft breast ready for cuddling and, more than that, a deep cave into which she could plunge her hand and pluck out body-warmed watermelon seeds to be pitted and eaten. Once, for almost a whole summer, while Caroline lay ill, it seemed there was only Wang Amah. Pearl slept with her nurse, burrowing under her arm, ate from her fingers, toddled in her shadow the whole day long. Once each day Wang Amah dressed the child carefully and then the two tip-toed to the sickroom and stood near the door so that Caroline, smiling wanly, eyes enormous in a wasted face, could see and wave.

Sometimes that summer Wang Amah was busy and Absalom Sydenstricker took over the job of dressing Pearl. She was restless and mischievous with Wang Amah but her father's rare and towering presence made her silent. His enormous hands fumbled at her clothing, never quite able to unravel the mystery of buttons or the nuisance of ribbons. Sometimes, while dressing Pearl, his eyes went blank and all movement stopped as he gave full attention to the new thought that had entered his mind and snatched him worlds away. The child squirmed silently until she was remembered again. When Absalom took her in to see her mother at last, Caroline laughed. "Oh, Absalom, you've buttoned her back in front again!"

"Oh, pshaw!" said Absalom absently. He and Pearl were both relieved when Wang Amah could at last swoop in to reclaim the child. Absalom disappeared into the room where he lived among his books and manuscripts.

When that summer was over Pearl had a new baby brother, Clyde, fat and blue-eyed and black-haired. Despite her struggle against dysentery Caroline had given birth to a round healthy baby. With cooler weather her strength returned. Once more her voice could be heard in the gatehouse and courtyard, the organ boomed joyfully, and excitement filled the house.

But not too much excitement—at least not while Absalom

was at home! Not that he was harsh; he was in manner a gentle man who rarely raised his voice and whose strongest oath was, "Oh, pshaw!" Yet under the gentleness glittered a will of steel, with a stubbornness of equal metal, and a fixed purpose that was a cannonball hurtling to its mark. Absalom was a missionary, a Presbyterian minister who felt it was his call to bring the Word of Christ to the Chinese. Everything else—food, clothing, family, money, comfort, pain, the upheavals of nations—all were of importance only to the extent they helped or hindered his Work. When the Work went well and souls were saved Absalom was radiant; when the Work fared badly his gloom cast a hush throughout the household.

Each morning when Absalom bent his head to ask grace before the breakfast meal Pearl could see three fiery marks on his forehead, as if branded there. They faded during the day, but in the morning they were back again. It took some time before Pearl Comfort summoned the courage to ask Caroline, "What makes the marks on Father's forehead?"

Caroline explained, "They are the marks of his fingers where he leans his head on his hand to pray. He prays for a whole hour every morning when he gets up."

There were no such marks on Caroline's forehead. "Why don't you pray, too, Mother?"

Caroline's answer had a sharp edge. "If I did, who would dress you and get breakfast and clean house and teach you your lessons? Some have to work, I suppose, while some pray."

Absalom's severe duties to God made the winter bleak, but in spring the household's mood changed. When the buds began to appear and the Yangtze River's tide, fattened by the mountain thaws, swelled the canals, then Absalom became especially restless and it seemed to him that all of China beckoned to him for salvation. He pored over his maps, planning journeys to new places where he could plant the Word of the Lord. At last, one spring morning turned out to be the day of his departure; the servants ran briskly to pack Absalom's things into a bedding roll; Caroline checked his clothing and saw that the roll was laid neatly over the white donkey's back. And Absalom, in pith helmet and light gray cotton suit, his face alight, his pockets filled with printed tracts and Bibles, scarcely remembered to say good-bye as he straddled the donkey and trotted away. The family and servants watched from the gate, waving to the stringy figure astride the comical little beast. Absalom's legs were so long his feet scraped the ground, and he held his cane, whose purpose was to beat off village dogs, like a lance. He disappeared past the willows around the bend. In the weeks to come he would travel incredible numbers of miles, braving wolves and storms and robbers, bringing his message to remote mountain villages where no white man had ever been before.

But behind him, at the house, a weight lifted. The servants gathered, chatted lazily. Edwin lounged. Caroline went to the organ and played and sang a long time, then curled up in a chair with a book. Pearl went out into the garden, and all the rest of that day she played there was no God. Caroline unknowingly helped that game because when evening came she took Pearl's hand and said, "We'll skip prayers tonight and take a walk instead—just for once God won't mind." At bedtime on one such night Pearl decided not to say her prayers at all and she lay awake in the dark a long time, frightened by her wickedness and quite positive God would punish her. But she was too stubborn to surrender. At last she fell asleep, her prayers still unsaid. She awoke, safe, to the golden sun of a summer morning. God had not punished her at all. Absalom was wrong.

One year Absalom decided that he wanted to penetrate even deeper into the interior of China and that it was therefore necessary to move the family to a new base farther north. With aching heart Caroline packed the clothing, wrapped matting around the furniture and the organ, dug up her precious roses, and made ready. Wang Amah had only to tie her few possessions into a bedding roll and a blue bandanna.

It turned out that in the new place the people were so hostile to foreigners that no one would rent them a house. The family took up quarters at last in a few rooms of a poor inn with earthen walls, a thatched roof, and beaten earth for a floor. It was in a thickly populated part of the town, and all about the missionary family throngs of ragged Chinese pressed closely, poverty-stricken, many homeless, many ill, almost all living in filth, and most of them unfriendly. Caroline could bear almost anything as long as there was space for a small garden, a breath of fresh air, and at least one or two others of her own kind. None of these was present in this new place. She set out her roses in pots and tried to find new ways of creating an American home for her children.

Absalom paid scant attention to such comforts or discomforts. The important thing for him was that he could now preach where no one else had yet gone. He often disappeared into the countryside for long stretches, unconcerned about hardship, danger, or the dark hostility of the people.

When winter came, the earthen house was cold and damp. When it rained, which was frequently, the earth floor welled with water, and Caroline had to make footpaths of brick and hoist the precious organ onto a platform. Her worst fears were realized when the baby Clyde caught a cold that developed into pneumonia. There was no doctor for hundreds of miles. Absalom was off on a preaching trip as usual. She hung blankets around the little sick boy, and she and Wang Amah worked unceasingly for ten days over the gasping child. He pulled through, but barely.

Caroline gathered her brood. "We will pack!" she declared. Again the roses were dug up from their pots, the furniture wrapped and tied in mats, the clothing set out in baskets and boxes. Everything ready, Caroline waited for Absalom's return. One early spring morning she saw him coming down the street, and at her signal the members of the family donned hats and coats, which had been held ready, and thus they met the astonished man of God.

"Enough!" Caroline told her husband. "You can preach from Peking to Canton, you can go from the North Pole to the South, but I and these little children will never go with you again. We are going back to Chinkiang and the bungalow on the hill, where there is peace and where there are hills and fresh air. I have offered up three children. I have no more children to give away to God now."

And with that she marched out the gate, holding Edwin by the hand, followed by Wang Amah carrying Clyde and holding Pearl's hand. Aware that nothing could prevail against Caroline's terrible wrath, Absalom could only bring up the rear of this small parade. Caroline led it to the edge of the canal, where she engaged a junk and porters to put their belongings aboard. After a journey of three weeks they were back in Chinkiang.

But Clyde was marked for death. One day when he was

five he became desperately ill with a high fever. Caroline feared diphtheria, but the Chinese-Indian doctor, whose medical skill was not the best, said it was bronchitis. The only other doctor in the city was the British customs doctor, but no one knew of his skill because no one had ever seen him sober. Clyde grew worse. Caroline sent a runner for her husband, who was three days away in the country. Before Absalom could make it back home the child suffocated. A fourth dead child lay in Caroline's arms, another sacrifice to China and God.

The day after Clyde was buried Pearl Comfort fell ill, and Caroline noted with dread the symptoms of the same disease that had taken Clyde. Where to go for help? The Indian doctor meant well, but he lacked knowledge. Caroline summoned a sedan chair, and thus borne by porters, she searched for the British port doctor. She found him in a bawdy house with a giggling Chinese girl on his knee. He was so drunk he could barely stand.

"My child is dying," Caroline told him. "It is diphtheria."

The physician made a great effort to summon his wits. He mumbled something about a new diphtheria vaccine he had picked up in Shanghai. He staggered to his feet and set off for his office, followed by Caroline in her sedan chair. She trailed him into his house, helped him find the small bottle and his hypodermic needle, aroused him when he sat down and began to nod, and kept him moving and awake until at last she had him at Pearl's bedside. The day after the injection Pearl was better, and after two doses she was out of danger.

And with that, Caroline had no more strength. She took to her bed, trembling and weak, at last giving way to the grief for Clyde she had not had time to vent. With mingled ache and hope she also felt new life stirring in her. Another baby was on the way. Wang Amah watched her mistress untiringly, brewed broths for her, slept like a dog by her door.

Edwin, ready for college, restless and friendless, was sent back to America and Uncle Cornelius' guiding hand. There was no one to take care of Pearl in her convalescence except Absalom, but the child turned her face from him and would not have him near. A British woman to whom Caroline had once been kind took over the job of nursing Pearl. Absalom did what he understood; he packed his bedroll, mounted his donkey, and trotted off into the hills to spread the Word of the Lord.

With spring came a baby sister for Pearl. Grace was her name.

Pearl, strong again, curious ever, neither confined by her older brother, who was absent, nor by her mother, who was busy, could venture out of the gates farther than ever before. She ranged through the town, to see what there was to see of China, her home.

Two

Foreign Devil

She knew she was an American and that she was white but she was never quite sure what that meant or how she was supposed to feel about it. She felt more Chinese than anything else, and her blonde hair caused her some embarrassment, for every sensible person in China knew that that was no color for hair to be. She and Wang Amah tried many ways of tucking up the blonde curls unseen under a little Buddha hat, but of course her blue eyes and fair skin gave her away. Every once in a while, a passerby on the street would hiss, "Foreign devil!" and she would know she was not Chinese.

Unlike other missionary families, the Sydenstrickers never considered that being white and American was in any sense better than being brown and Chinese. Absalom and Caroline despised the arrogance of other missionaries and traders and fought against it all their lives. Although Caroline was desperately homesick for her family and country, and she strove mightily to maintain American values and attitudes in her children, it was more to keep alive the links with the beloved homeland than from any attitude of superiority. Absalom's passion for what he believed to be the true faith and his determination to bring that faith to the Chinese did not, he felt, give him any special privileges.

Pearl's father had contempt only for stupid and boorish persons, and these came in all colors. He was too much a scholar to bother with such nonsense as racial superiority, although it seemed quite logical to him to believe that women were inferior to men. As soon as he arrived in China, he plunged into a study of the Chinese language, which he found rich, and Chinese literature and history, which he found deep and satisfying. He studied Buddhism intently and saw many resemblances in it to Christianity. For a period he even grew a pigtail and wore Chinese robes until even he could see that, with his lank blond six feet of length, they only made him look ridiculous. He prided himself on the perfection of his Chinese accent and the classic style of his speech.

Pearl's first language was Chinese. As a small child, she spent most of her time in the company of Wang Amah or playing with neighboring children. English was the language of more formal events, the tongue she spoke with her parents. That all seemed quite right to her. In the morning she worked at lesson assignments given her by her mother—English grammar, American and world history, arithmetic. There were also, of course, the music lessons given her by Caroline, but the language of music was international. And from her mother she heard stories about America, its places and people, and she quickened to the yearning in her mother's voice and moist eyes. But after lunch divided her day, she became Chinese. Then her Chinese tutor came, a man quite long in dignity and pigtail, to instruct her in Chinese reading and writing. From him she learned the sayings of the philosopher Confucius, the history of China, and the proper forms of Chinese behavior.

She loved to hear about the Empress Dowager Tsu Hsi, the fierce old lady who still ruled China from her great palace in Peking. Eagerly she listened to how this Manchu princess, descended from the Manchurian overlords who had long ago conquered China, had come to the emperor's court as a beautiful maiden of sixteen. She had been selected by the monarch to be one of his many concubines. For most girls so selected, it meant that they would be kept forever isolated from the world in the palace harem, forgotten even by the emperor. But this young woman was too beautiful, clever, and ambitious for such a fate. She persuaded powerful courtiers to help her win her way to the emperor's side. She became his favorite concubine, and, when she bore him a son, she became his wife and an empress in truth. When the emperor died, she assumed control with the aid of a brilliant and handsome general. Her own son died, and she ruled firmly, stopping at nothing to defend her power, not even at imprisoning her nephew, the next in line to the throne, when he became a threat to her.

So Pearl spent her lesson days learning about two worlds in two languages. But she was quick at her studies, and despite this double learning life, she had a great deal of time to herself.

She roamed the neighborhood, where she was an accepted member of the younger set in the merry, noisy Chinese households. She joined in their hilarity over the antics of the white settlement. There was the dignified American who kept a hidden whiskey bottle in his closet. Another woman would not sleep with her husband, and one lonely young American man tried to make love to every passing Chinese woman. There was the arrogant missionary who was so bad-tempered no Chinese would work for him, except one old lady. This servant survived because she achieved her revenge every morning by leaning out of her attic window and emptying her chamberpot on the roof, which drained down to the rain cistern from which the old man, who distrusted the Chinese wells, took his drinking water.

After the laughter, some kind old Chinese member of the family would say, "But the Christians are good, nevertheless. They do their best and we must not blame them for what they do not know. After all, they were not born Chinese. Heaven did not ordain." All would agree gravely, including Pearl, sponging into her mind everything that was being said.

She wandered the city. Down the hill toward the river she would go, perhaps to stop at the Buddhist temple and, if the hour was right, listen to the bell. It was a great bronze bell hanging in a frame, and it made a soul-stirring sound. When she was smaller she had been afraid of its sad voice in the night. But now she could watch as a little old priest with a kind face came to the bell, carrying an enormous club wrapped in cloth. He swung mightily against the bell and the pure sound rolled out, lapping like surf against the ears, heart, and mind. She loved that sound; it was the voice of China, and at the same time a voice that spoke darkly of the world beyond China and of that universe of the spirit that was beyond all of it.

Then farther down the hill to the Bund, the street that ran along the Yangtze River. Here great hulks of ships lay, taking on or discharging cargo, swarmed over by endless lines of Chinese laborers, the coolies, who carried on their backs the great sacks of Java sugar, rice, jute, seeds, and spices. Their legs quivered and the sweat poured from them as they bent under their loads and the curses of the foremen. On the river, barges and sailing junks and sampans glided past anchored British and American gunboats. Ferries laden with humanity bustled back and forth between the Chinkiang side, where Pearl was, and the far shore, where crouched the city of Yangchow, once governed by Marco Polo.

The river itself was a thing of fascination and terror. Broad, powerful, mud-yellow, it swept by. From its depths treacherous undercurrents boiled to the surface. Frequently, to get from an offshore river steamer to the shore meant a transfer from the steamer to a bobbing sampan that could move across the shallow flats. It was a dangerous moment, for a slip could cause a spill into the river, from which there was no escape, so unrelenting was the current. More than once Pearl watched horror-stricken as someone slipped into the yellow maw of the river and was instantly gone. No one even attempted rescue. Once, in a storm, she saw a ferry roll over, dumping its passengers into the water. Hundreds of black bobbing heads could be seen for a moment or two, and then they disappeared.

Pearl knew that the reason no one tried to rescue these victims was not only because it was dangerous but because the Chinese had a cruel superstition that prevented many from putting out a hand even to save a threatened child. The river was believed to be the instrument of the gods, who decreed who was to live and who to die. A person saved from the death the gods wanted for him would only go on to commit some terrible crime—and the person who had saved him and thus defied the gods would then be responsible.

China was a world built around the acceptance of fate. There was something terrible in this acceptance, and it made Pearl angry, for it seemed to her the Chinese accepted and endured more than they had to. But some of that Chinese accept-ance—the part that was pure patience—entered and became part of her. She learned how to wait.

And she learned death. She had seen her younger brother Clyde die and she herself had been snatched narrowly from death. She knew of the three others in their little graves in Shanghai. In some of the Chinese homes she visited there was a bright black varnished coffin standing ready for the oldest member of the family, who had ordered it made exactly the way he wanted it. It was a cherished and familiar piece of furni-ture in the household and the owner guarded his coffin care-fully to see that the children did not scratch it in their play. If he were offended in a family quarrel he might even climb into his coffin to show his hurt or spite, emerging only after a dutiful apology. When at last he died he would be put into the coffin, perhaps in a bright red shroud, and the lid would be nailed shut, and there he might sleep for weeks or months, the family life swirling about him, until some day chosen for luck, prefer-ably in the summer when the weather was pleasant, when he would be buried in his coffin among his ancestors in the cemetery.

Pearl was fond of funerals. When she saw a funeral pro-cession, the mourners dressed in white, she joined it and watched. At the grave, incense was lighted, a white cock was killed and its blood spilled, and there was much burning of bright paper pictures of men, women, house, furniture, and money. The mourners were curious about the little blonde foreigner who watched them so gravely and they took it for granted that she could speak only in a foreign tongue. Some-times her presence started off talk about foreigners. She heard them say, "The foreigners take the eyes out of babies to make pills to cure malaria," or "Foreigners are opposite to us in all ways. They are born with white hair and die with black."

Once she could take no more of this and said aloud, in Chinese, "Everything you say is lies."

It caused a sensation. One old grandmother, who could not conceive of the sound of Chinese coming from such a face, cried out, "Ai-ya, I am going to die! I can understand the talk of foreign devils!"

Then came the questions. Did everyone in her country look like her? What kind of underwear did she wear? What kind of food was eaten in her country? Were foreign babies made in the same way as Chinese babies? This last question baffled her; although she never had any doubt how Chinese babies were made, for the most intimate details of this were openly discussed in Chinese homes she knew, she had never heard from Caroline how it was done in America.

When the burial was of an old person who had been ready for death, the funeral was generally a cheerful event. The actual death had probably occurred weeks or months previously anyway. But sometimes it was obvious that a beloved person had died prematurely, and the grief of the mourners struck her to the soul. She fled the scene, weeping, to throw herself on some other grave and there to cry alone for reasons she did not understand.

And for a time she took up a lonely battle against death. It was after the family moved from the house near the river to a cottage in the hills outside the city. Poor Chinese families rarely buried dead babies; the little bodies were wrapped in matting and thrown away in the hills. Most of these were baby girls, for in Chinese families with many children a girl baby was sometimes strangled at birth, before she could cry and

suckle and engage the family's love. Pearl, exploring one day
the hills and the city walls, came upon a place where the hill-
side was strewn with fragments of tiny bodies, worried at and
mangled by packs of half-wild dogs. Little hands, arms, and
legs lay separated from the bodies. Horror-stricken, she began
to run away and then stopped, haunted by one doll-like face.
She went back and, in a rage, chased away the dogs with a
stick. She fell to her knees and wept, then dug a hole with the
stick, lined it with grass, tenderly buried the bits and pieces of
unwanted babies, and sprinkled wild flowers over the mounds.
She went back there many times, carrying a grass-woven bag
in which to collect her sad burdens and a club with which to
fight off the dogs. When she saw dogs hunched over some
object in those hills, she flew at them, a small blonde avenging
spirit, and buried the tiny bodies, sometimes only a skull or a
bone, each with something bright—a piece of gay-colored glass
or porcelain or a flower. And she never told anyone about it.
From then on she could never learn to love dogs.

Life, love, birth, death—great events were very close to
the surface of Pearl's different worlds. She watched, listened,
stirred by the mighty forces they represented.

One day her father came back from one of his expeditions
into the hills with a strange tale to tell. He had set out deliberately to find a bandit chieftain who was terrorizing the
countryside. Absalom had simply walked into the mountain
temple where the robber band had taken up headquarters and
he had spoken to the chief about religion. The man was an
ex-soldier famous for his exploits in war but forced to flee the
army when he killed his superior officer. He was well educated
and talked intelligently about many things, courteous and
gentle in his manner. And just as courteously he explained to

Absalom that he robbed and killed not for money but simply for the excitement of it. Once the army had instilled in him the thrill of killing, everything else bored him. So he had left his wife and children to become an outlaw. He enjoyed watching people die. It gave him a sense of power. Smiling, he told Absalom all this.

"More than we know," Caroline murmured, "that is the explanation of war." She caught sight of Pearl then and ordered her to bed. But the child had heard it all and it stayed with her. What was that terrible animal urge to violence and death in man? How complicated, how dark, how strange and fierce were people's hearts, how deep the current of life! And what a great thing it would be to be able to capture it all on paper, to weave tales that were as strong and rich and outrageous as life itself—ah, that would be true power, to put life into a capsule of paper!

There were not many models of how that could be done. The Bible, of course, was a boiling tide of life, but she was forced to read it not as a collection of rousing tales and a catalogue of man's vices and virtues but as holy print, large sections of which were to be memorized to the point of stupor. Books for children were not easily available. Novels were considered frivolous and immoral by both Mr. Kung and her parents.

Caroline had a weakness, nevertheless; she was ashamed of it but gave in to it. The weakness was for Dickens, and it led her at one time to buy a set of the English writer's complete works, which she placed high on the top shelf where the children could not reach it.

She counted without Pearl's curiosity and agility. One day when she was seven Pearl climbed the shelves and plucked out *Oliver Twist*. She read it through, weeping, snorting, laughing. She was stunned. She had no idea books could be like this. She read it again, immediately. And then, one by one, she devoured all the other books in the set and, in the years that followed, tracked to their hiding places the other novels Caroline read secretly, to Absalom's disgust. Despite herself, Caroline could not resist a good story, either. It became a silent and gentle contest between mother and daughter, but later it occurred to Pearl that Caroline's hiding places for novels were a bit too easy to find to be entirely serious.

Three

✤

Rebellion!

For many years now, indeed all through her reign, the Empress Dowager had watched in rage while foreigners nibbled away at her empire. England was the worst offender, followed closely and hungrily by Germany, France, Russia, and Japan. In later years the United States had also become interested in China. These foreign nations demanded the right to travel freely in China, bring in goods for sale, seize large territories, and send their missionaries to convert the Chinese to Christianity. To enforce their demands they sent soldiers, warships, and guns. The empress's troops, fighting with primitive weapons, melted before the awful killing power of the foreign guns. The Chinese had never developed artillery or warships. The Europeans even won a war enforcing their "right" to import and sell opium, an extremely profitable product, to the Chinese, who were well on their way toward becoming a nation of drug addicts.

"They are carving us up like a melon!" the Empress Dowager groaned.

She decided in the year 1900 to make one last desperate effort to free her empire from the white grip. She also needed a cause that would unite her people and direct some of their anger away from her own squandering of tax moneys. The fierce old lady, superstitious and ignorant of the ways of war, sought help from the Boxers, a secret society of terrorists who claimed they had such magical powers no European bullets could pierce their skins. Perhaps she believed them, perhaps she only hoped that these desperate men would help awaken the numb resentment of the Chinese and start a great uprising that would throw the foreigner out. She ordered that all foreigners must leave China forever, and she commanded her governors and the Boxers to kill all white persons who dared to stay on Chinese soil.

Even before that fearful order the Sydenstrickers, like all whites in China, could sense the gathering storm. Their Chinese neighbors became less friendly, and now and then in the street a Chinese would look at them in open hatred, spitting as they passed, showing a resentment that would have not been dared before, so feared was the white man. Absalom came home from his expeditions more dejected each time, and he began to spend hours at home with apparently nothing to do. He confessed that he was being forced to close up many of the chapels he had established; their landlords had suddenly refused to rent space.

One night Absalom did not come home. He appeared at noon the next day, bruised and haggard, his wrists bleeding. He had been administering Communion to the dying mother of Lin Meng, a convert. Soldiers had come, bound Absalom by his wrists to a post, and then had taken away Lin Meng and his ten-year-old son. Thus bound, praying, he had watched the old woman die. At midday the boy had returned and untied Absalom, telling how the soldiers had tortured Lin Meng to death. Relating this to his family, Absalom exclaimed, "Lin Meng has entered the presence of our Lord, a martyr, to stand among that glorified host!" and then he went into his study and shut the door.

Rumors began coming in. In one small town in the province of Shantung every member of the little missionary group had been slaughtered, including the children and babies. Missionaries and their families began filtering in from the interior, their passage aided by secret friends among the Chinese. They told tales of narrow escapes from the soldiers and Boxers who hunted them. Babies had died of illness along the long and desperate marches. Caroline cared for these starved and ragged refugees and then sent them to safety in Shanghai, where the white community was armed and powerful.

The Sydenstrickers made plans for escape. They rehearsed a secret route from their house in the hills down through the thick bamboos and valley ponds to the riverside. They arranged with the American consul that should he suspect treachery, he would fire a cannon and fly a red flag from the pole high over the consulate. Near the door they kept ready a small basket of food, extra shoes for each person, and changes of underwear rolled together. Caroline buried a few valuables in a hole dug in the cellar.

And they waited. But Absalom decided that, if the signal came, he would not leave. He would stay behind to give courage to his flock and share their fate. Wasn't he afraid to die? "It is not death one fears," said Absalom, in love with God. But Caroline was afraid of death for her children and she would take them away when danger threatened.

The cannon boomed one August afternoon and the red flag whipped to the top of the consulate flagpole. With sinking hearts the family hastened down the escape route to the riverside, where they boarded a river steamer that was ready.

Caroline, Pearl, Grace, and Wang Amah stood on the deck, and, as the craft cast off, turned to wave good-bye. Absalom stood, a lone forlorn figure, looking ridiculously foreign in his white suit and pith helmet, tall and white among the small brown people around him. At his side was the Arab, Ma, a Muslim whom Absalom had converted to Christianity and who believed him to be a saint. Would they see him again?

Pearl did not wonder about that long, for she was soon caught up in the excitement of the river voyage. There was the ship, captained by a glowering Scot, to explore and there were the wonders of the green banks of the river and the busy ports. One night she lay in her berth listening to someone on deck play a two-stringed Chinese violin. The melody twisted like a wisp of smoke, impossible to duplicate and yet impossible to forget. It was one of the many voices of her China.

But, China was not hers. She was a "foreign devil," a hated invader. She was an American. Her land, known only in her mother's tales, was across the sea.

"Take me to America, to our country," she begged Caroline.

"Not yet," Caroline said quietly, looking up the river from whence they had come.

They got off the steamer at Shanghai, a thunderously busy port where warships of America and Europe lay in the harbor. Caroline found a small three-room flat on a quiet street and there began the wait for word from Absalom. Pearl and Grace discovered for the first time the luxury of a built-in bathtub and real faucets—water coming right out of the wall! Back in Chinkiang they had bathed in a tin tub filled with buckets of water brought in by water-bearers. Down the street she found two English girls, their skin like milk, dressed in starched frocks. She felt awkward with her scraped knees and sun-burned face. But the girls politely played with her, and they taught the little savage to skip rope.

Pearl's lessons, now conducted wholly by Caroline, were in English. More and more, the subjects had to do with America, its land and history. Caroline's longing for home was intense, and Pearl listened to the tales of America with a different kind of attentiveness, for now Caroline's yearning had become hers. Again she heard the story of America's gentle wooded hills, aflame in autumn and veiled in green gauze in the spring, and the fields bursting with crops in summer. How fine to leap on a horse and go galloping down the fields as Caroline had done! How marvelous it would be to go there and find one's place among the aunts and uncles and cousins, and feel oneself part of a long human chain emerging out of the far past and stretching on to unknown futures.

One day Pearl and Caroline were walking along a crowded narrow street. It was hot and the crowds seemed to make the heat even more intense. Ahead of them ambled a large Chinese gentleman, quite broad in the beam, blocking the way. It was impossible to get past him, and he moved so slowly! His long pigtail, tied with a woven black-silk cord and ending in a large tassel, swayed like a pendulum behind his back. On an impulse Pearl yanked the tassel gently, as a signal to walk a little faster. The man whirled around and gave Pearl a look of such wrath and hatred that ice seized her heart.

Caroline paled. "Please forgive her," she begged. "She is only a child and I will punish her."

The man stalked away. Caroline pulled Pearl down another street. "Don't ever do anything like that again," she warned. "It is dangerous."

This was not just a case of bad manners or misdirected mischief, Pearl understood. This was something new, told in the Chinese gentleman's open hatred and in Caroline's frightened face. It was part of what was happening all over China, and indeed, it was why she was in Shanghai. But why such hatred? Did every Chinese feel it?

Her Confucian teacher had once told her that Chinese were exploited by white men. She was not quite sure what exploitation meant, but she connected it with the long swarms of sweat-drenched coolies, bent double under their burdens, toiling along the wharves like ants, clutching the tally sticks they had to present for meager pay to the Englishman sitting in a chair under an umbrella.

The Boxer Rebellion was squashed in short order. The foreign powers rapidly sent gunboats and troops. An expeditionary force of soldiers from Britain, France, Italy, Germany, Austria, Russia, United States, and Japan marched swiftly on the Peking home of the Empress Dowager herself. The Empress Dowager and her court fled the Imperial Palace. Her troops were helpless against the superior guns and training of the invaders. When a treaty was signed at last, it made China a subject nation, with nearly unlimited rights for foreigners to do as they wished inside her borders. Also, China had to pay a stiff tax to cover the cost of maintaining foreign troops on her soil.

Small wonder, then, that the end of the rebellion itself did not spell the end of resentment against the white invaders. Indeed the unfair, cruel terms of the settlement deepened the hatred. Chinese who had formerly observed the whites with amusement became sullen and angry. They were losing the habits of patience and tolerance that had stood them in such good stead for centuries.

So it was that Absalom, who had weathered the eight months safely in Chinkiang, could see no improvement when the peace treaty was signed. The chapels he had established in better days continued to close down one by one. Two were burned to the ground. The people refused to listen to talk about a foreign god. When Absalom appeared in their villages the dogs were set on him, stones were thrown at him, and he was spat on.

One day he turned up in Shanghai and stood in the doorway of the apartment. His children had nearly forgotten him, but there he stood, taller than they remembered, and leaner, and far more piercing of eye. Never affectionate, he was now nearly tongue-tied by his shyness with his children and did not know what to say to them.

As far as Pearl was concerned, he had only one important thing to say and he said it. "We are going to take a year off and go to America!" he said.

Four

❧

"A Country of My Own"

The ship steamed through the Golden Gate passage and there, to starboard, San Francisco's white houses marched up and down the hills. The city looked so clean. The smell was so different from that in China, more of food than of dung, more of sawn wood than of incense.

One big surprise came when the ship docked and Pearl watched the stevedores move to their tasks of unloading baggage and cargo. How big and muscular they were! "Even the coolies here are white!" she exclaimed.

Caroline laughed. "We don't have coolies in our country," she explained. "Everybody works here, and it's no disgrace to work with your hands." Then she gave Pearl and Grace a sharper look, worrying because her children were so strongly influenced by the Orient. That very year, she resolved, she would teach them to cook, sew, wash dishes, and do housework. "We Americans *work!*" she told Pearl.

They crossed the United States by rail, hardly taking their eyes away from the windows even to eat. Caroline was their guide, pointing out each new aspect of life in America and how it had changed in the years since she had last been home. The rolling train smelled of green plush and sharp cinders. It clacked and tooted across the desert, the Rocky Mountains, the vast plains, the fat farmlands, the mighty cities with their millions of lights and towering buildings. Now and then the railroad tracks paralleled a road, and they could see one of the new-fangled automobiles, its passengers scarved and goggled, vainly trying to keep up with the train. On this trip Pearl and Grace ate ice cream for the first time.

At last they were home in West Virginia. An uncle met them at the station and loaded them and their baggage into a carriage drawn by two fat horses. And all the way down the road it was just as Caroline had pictured it to Pearl—the heavy trees and deep shade, the gentle green meadows. The carriage stopped under the maple trees while the big white gate swung open, and there at the end of the wide lawn was home. Caroline's house stood solid and square and white, with vine-covered pillars supporting a portico. This was the house in which she had been born, thought Pearl, and it was all exactly the way it was in her mind, and wasn't that strange? Was it so familiar because of Caroline's stories or did she actually remember it?

And who was that white-haired man coming to greet the carriage—Could that be Grandfather Hermanus? No, it was Caroline's oldest brother, Cornelius, grown gray in her absence. Behind him now, the erect little man with the shock of silver hair, neat as buttons in black silk suit and snowy linen—*that* was her grandfather and he seemed the oldest man Pearl had ever seen. She dashed into the house. The parlor was to the left and the library to the right, of course. Then up the stairs with the hand-carved balustrade, and the important room, the room in which she was born, would be at the front of the house, to the left, overlooking the lawn and the sun-dappled tree. She knew exactly where to go. There was the broad old-fashioned bed the way it was supposed to be, but something seemed missing—a table, a chest?

"I remember when I was born. I am sure I remember!" she thought.

The family did not stay long in Grandfather Hermanus' house but went on to Lexington, Virginia, to be near Edwin, who was a student at Washington and Lee University. How tall and scholarly he looked, with his rimless glasses! They rented a house with a big stone fireplace and stayed there for the rest of the winter and part of the following summer. Here Pearl went to school, but remembered nothing about it later except that her mother's tutoring had put her so far ahead of the other children her age that there was little for her to do in school.

In a Virginia wood that winter she saw snow for the first time. Caroline rubbed pine needles in her hands and held them to her nose and closed her eyes, as if drunk on the fragrance, and cried out, "Oh, America—its lovely, lovely *smell!*"

In midsummer they returned to her grandfather's house in West Virginia and its marvelous abundance of aunts, uncles, and cousins. Here was pure joy, for Pearl learned to ride a horse, ate all the grapes and other fruit she could pick, mowed the hay and tumbled in the wagons, churned butter, and quite often simply ran through the meadows as fast as she could just because she felt so good.

She could not get over the wonder that there were no fences around the fields or walls around the house. Here people felt safe, and it seemed there was no war or hatred. It shook her then, when one hot September day Hermanus urgently summoned the family into the library and announced, "Children, the President of the United States has been assassinated. President McKinley is dead."

Pearl broke into tears, crying out, "Oh, must we have the revolution here, too?"

"What in the world is the child talking about?" demanded Hermanus. Nobody knew except Caroline, who let Pearl cry it out on her shoulder.

And then, all too soon, the year was up, and it was time to return to China. Absalom fidgeted to get back to his work and put to use the sums of money he had collected in America. He, of course, never thought of what he was leaving, for his soul was in China. Caroline must have ached to leave the place she loved so dearly, yet it was easier this time than nine years before, because she had seen now that there was no place remaining for her at home; her sisters and brothers were grown and filling out their lives without her, and even her father, whom she would probably never see again, had grown accustomed to her absence, and her friends were scattered and strangers. Even Edwin was fashioning his own life, and she was not a part of it.

The year had been the most important in Pearl's life. One day she would say of that year: "I had seen him [her grandfather], I had lived in the house with him, I had felt him the source of my being, because he was my mother's father, and his other children were my uncles and aunts and their children were my cousins, and so I was one of a clan and not solitary. No, we were Americans, and I had a country of my own, and a big white house where my kinfolk lived, and there were generations of us there, all belonging together. So a child ought to feel, and if he so feels, he can wander to and fro upon the earth and never walk alone."

They came back to a strangely quiet China. The white man's guns and armies had spread fear. They were now allowed to come and go as they liked, to trade as they wished, to send missionaries anywhere. And no Chinese dared lift a finger against them, for it was said that if one but looked crossly at the white man his punishment would be swift and terrible. So powerful had Europeans become in China and so complete was the collapse of the Empress Dowager's influence that now many Chinese sought to gain the white man's favor and to join his churches, because that gave them influence and power. No Chinese judge dared harm a Chinese who had become a Christian and thus put himself under the white man's protection.

But there were warnings, and Pearl heard one of them from her gentle Confucian teacher, Mr. Kung, whose family home in Peking had been ransacked and destroyed by Germans. "It will be peaceful for you here again, Little Sister, but not for long. The storm is still rising and when it breaks you must be far away from here. You must go to America and stay there and not come back, lest next time you be killed with all your kind."

"There must be a next time?"

"Until justice is done!"

And Pearl wept. She and her family were not like the others, she felt, and it was terrible that this would make no difference at all.

But Absalom saw only that Chinese were flocking to join the church. He did not ask why. He saw the change only as a triumph for God. He doubled his traveling and preaching, and rejoiced. He opened new churches by the dozen, trained new preachers by the score, and began new schools. It did not take long before he presided over more than two hundred churches, each with a school.

Caroline knew. She was closer to the common people, and many confided in her. She could see that many of those now hastening to become Christians were sped not by their love of God but by a greater love for money and influence. Always, in every society, there would be those to lick the boots of the mighty, and the white man and his church had become mighty in China. She told Absalom about one of his preachers who was making a fortune charging money for admission to his church, of another who secretly kept three concubines, and of yet another who sold opium. Absalom scoffed at it all as women's gossip. Besides, he said, it was God's job, not his, to select the good souls from the bad. His job was merely to bring them to the church in greater numbers, whatever their motives.

And Pearl watched, listened, and began to shape her own mind. She felt alone, but she was not particularly sad about that; she simply accepted it as the way it was. Something in her withdrew from this passion over God, which she could neither prove nor disprove, and instead was drawn to truths about people, which she could see for herself.

She saw that the way of the world ran strong even among the missionaries, who claimed to be above it all. She knew of the gentle, white-haired old preacher whose thirst for women was so intense that he brought into his house a fresh young country girl as his mistress, while his aging wife helped him keep it a secret. And she knew the Chinese pastor who numbered among his children a pale one with brown hair and gray eyes; when the full story came out it appeared that this pastor had lent his wife to his white superior, whose own wife was away in America.

"The white man who is my chief lives a very lonely life," explained the pastor, "and did not David take another man's wife, yet he was the Lord's beloved?"

And what was the undertow of life, she wondered, to explain the bent old missionary who, after forty years of marriage and work together, suddenly left his home and declared he loathed his wife, shouting, "I don't ever want to hear her voice again!"

Or how did one explain the secret locked for years in one seemingly pleasant missionary family: the man would get moods of madness in which he would seize a knife and attempt to kill his wife, then make her crawl on hands and knees, yet the wife never told and swore her children to secrecy.

Pearl knew the story, too, of the missionary's wife who, after bearing eight children, leaped from her bed one night and raced through the streets in her nightgown to plunge from a cliff into the Yangtze River. To match this was the story of another missionary wife, pretty and Southern and vivacious, who also rose from her bed one night and tried to cut her throat with a carving knife but did not die, and then tried to hang herself but the rope broke, and then crawled to the bathroom and found poison and managed to die at last, all while her husband and four little children slept.

So many of these missionaries and their families, their own affairs in turmoil and their passions aflame, yet lived tight little lives, narrow and mean. They hated China and its people and language and closed their minds to any idea that might stir them. One such man, finding Pearl reading a book on evolution, roared at her, "I would no more think of reading a book against my belief, or of talking with an unbeliever except to preach to him, than I would think of taking poison into my body!"

Romantically dreaming over a love poem by Tennyson, Pearl looked up one day to ask, "Mother, were you and Father ever in love?"

There was a look of sudden fright, of a secret suddenly naked, on Caroline's face. And then Caroline snapped the secret shut. "Your father and I have both been very busy people," she said too briskly. "We have thought of our duty rather than how we felt."   75-104

It sorrowed Pearl that there was so much pain in living. Each person, it seemed, carried about in his heart a lonely secret, a hurt, a disappointment, an unspent wish, a driving desire for what was not at hand. She learned the ways by which such secrets left their traces in people's eyes, gestures, turns of speech. And what a boiling stew of humanity, each person and his private hurts blown like a leaf by winds that swept such leaves into piles! The Boxer Rebellion had been such a wind, and then a few years after her return from the United States, she witnessed another, even more devastating.

For famine had pounced on China. Bad weather had ruined the crops of the north, even in the rich Yangtze valley. Starvation stalked the land. Wretched peasants in rags began streaming south by the hundreds of thousands. The roadsides were lined with corpses, crooked hands frozen skyward still begging food. Hungry men, women, and children thronged into the cities, lay in streets and doorways, built crude packing-crate shelters against the walls, and begged piteously for crumbs.

In that terrible year the Sydenstrickers did all they could.

Absalom went deep into the north, where the famine was worst, to take charge of administering relief funds sent from America. What few dollars he could spare he sent to Caroline, who dressed herself in rags and with Wang Amah went among the people quietly to drop a dollar here and a food bundle there. Her life was endangered by this action, for if she were to be discovered in the act of giving, the beggars might have fallen on her and fought for what she had. Yet her identity became known and beggars crept in great numbers up the hill and beat on the gates and lay shivering against the walls. All night long they moaned her name and by morning some were dead and had to be carted away.

Not that year the fun of opening the crate of Christmas gifts ordered from the Montgomery Ward catalogue. Every penny went for food for the hungry. Even Absalom's pet project, the translation of the Bible from Greek into Mandarin Chinese, which had always consumed so much of the family's funds, went unattended. Caroline and Pearl themselves went begging to houses in the white settlement, pleading for money and food to give to the starving. When one relief ship brought in hundreds of cheeses—a food never eaten by Chinese and one they could not tolerate—Caroline begged the whites to buy the cheeses, and with the money she bought flour and rice for the needy.

By spring the crisis had worn off. Those who survived took again to the roads, this time to return home and attempt to plant and start over. But the horror of it could never be forgotten, nor could its terrible questions be far from Pearl's mind. Why did God permit such things? Why must humans suffer so? Caroline could see these questions in Pearl's face, and she worried about this solitary daughter of hers with the face that had become so grave. In just another few years it would be time to send Pearl to college, and no one could be less ready than she to take up life in the company of American girls. In preparation, and in order to give Pearl some needed experience with her own kind, Caroline decided to send her to a boarding school in Shanghai.

Five

But Where Is Home?

Miss Jewell's boarding school in Shanghai was in a forbidding gray fortress of a building, dimly lit, its windows heavily barred. Miss Jewell floated noiselessly through the rooms on soft-soled shoes, her sharp black eyes noting everything.

The teachers at the school were generally good, but Pearl learned little from them. In most subjects, thanks to her mother's imaginative teaching and her own love of reading, she was far ahead of the other girls. Studying in classes bored her and she found such subjects as Latin and math actually painful.

At first she shared an attic room with two other girls, also the daughters of missionaries. But these girls had been bred on the notion that whites were superior and the Chinese somehow less than human. They knew only enough Chinese words to give orders to servants, although they had lived in China all their lives, and they were dumbfounded by Pearl because of the letters in Chinese she wrote to her friends. They were horrified by Pearl's insistence that Chinese civilization, philosophy, and religion deserved study and respect. When Pearl discussed Buddhism and noted its similarities to Christianity, her roommates reported her to Miss Jewell as a heretic. Pearl was moved out of the attic and into a room of her own so that she would not contaminate the others. She liked it better that way, for now she could read long after the others were asleep. She wrote poems and stories, and even began a novel.

Miss Jewell decided that the heretic needed a strong dose of religion, and so she took Pearl on Sundays to strange ceremonies in dark halls filled with moaning, praying, shrieking worshippers begging to be forgiven for their sins. Pearl was terrified. She had no idea what kind of sect this was. Even though religion played a strong role in her own family and training, it was not this hysterical sort, and her father's sermons suffered more from scholarly dryness than from talk of damnation and hellfire. She wrote home, and her alarmed parents immediately ordered that on Sundays she be taken only to the Community Church, where a round little English preacher gave brief and sober sermons.

But Miss Jewell had other ways of saving Pearl's soul, and one of these was to see that her student became involved in "good works." Miss Jewell's notion of good works was to help people who had reached the dregs of life, and she seemed to have a talent for finding the very bottom. One of her charities was the Door of Hope, a rescue home for Chinese slave girls who had been mistreated. It was Pearl's job to teach these girls how to sew and knit. It was not uncommon, especially in hard times, for poor Chinese to sell a daughter and sometimes even a son to a rich family. This brought in money for food, and for the young girl it frequently meant a chance to avoid certain starvation. If the family were kind as well as rich, the bondmaid would live well as a favored servant and at eighteen she would be given her freedom and married off. But it also happened that these poor girls wound up in cruel families, where they were whipped by their mistresses and badly used by the men in the household. At the Door of Hope, the mistreated slave girls were fed, helped to freedom, and encouraged to train themselves for household jobs.

Pearl, who spoke Chinese as fluently as a native, heard these poor creatures tell tales of cruelty and evil that kept her awake and sobbing many a night. She learned how some mistresses tortured their slave girls with burning coals and cigarettes, how slave traders ranged the provinces in hard times hunting and buying the children of starving families for profitable sale to rich city folk. In her experiences so far she had known many hard realities of life and learned how to accept them, but even her experience of death, hunger, and rebellion had not prepared her for such deliberate wickedness of the mighty against the weak.

But she was to learn more before the year was out. Another one of Miss Jewell's good works, into which she recruited Pearl, was connected with a shelter for prostitutes. The sensitive young girl was horror-stricken by these women who had sunk to the lowest depths. These women of her own race, white women of every Western nation, French, English, German, Belgian, American, were so sunk in poverty and disease and loneliness that they seemed far worse off than the slave girls at the Door of Hope. For once, Pearl's ability to communicate with all kinds of people found its limits, and there was no way for her to understand these wretches or talk with them. She could pity the slave girls, who had been forced into their unhappy lot, but the prostitutes seemed to have made a deliberate choice of this gutter of life, and nothing in Pearl's seventeen years prepared her for sympathy with such a choice. It frightened her to deal with them. She grew pale and thin.

When she went home for spring holidays and told Caroline and Absalom of her "good works," she knew that would be the end of boarding school, and it was. It was decided that she would enter an American college that fall and that the family would take another vacation in order to deliver her there, for it was already time for Absalom to have another furlough. Eight years had passed quickly since that last journey home.

Not that Absalom was eager to take a vacation. Taking time off from his work seemed immoral to him, and he hated to spend money on anything but his missions and fresh editions of the New Testament he had translated into Chinese. He was shocked to discover the cost of sending Pearl to college, and even went so far as to write a rich man he knew to ask if he would care to pay the cost of educating a budding missionary.

When Pearl found out about this she wept with anger and shame. "He doesn't need to feed me!" she told Caroline, "I'll leave college and get a job. I can look out for myself."

"Try to understand," Caroline begged. "He isn't like other men. He's like somebody in a dream."

But Caroline had stood up to Absalom before, and she did so again. She cornered him in their bedroom, from which Pearl could hear a muted but violent argument going on for some time. When it was over, Absalom emerged thoughtful and crestfallen, but Caroline was bright-eyed. "You will go to college," she told Pearl triumphantly, "and you will get a new dress, and we shall go home by way of Europe and see the world!"

Caroline bought a trunkful of books on Europe, and the family read them during the steamer journey up the Yangtze River to Hankow, the train trip to Peking, and then to Harbin in Manchuria, from where they embarked on the long railway journey across Siberia. There was little room on the train for Absalom's long legs, and he sat stiff and melancholy for most of the trip while Pearl, Grace, and Caroline glued their noses to the window and watched the wild landscape slide by.

Then they were in Russia, and here they were struck by the contrast between wealth and poverty in that unhappy land. They saw nobles and priests surrounded by kingly wealth. The vast cathedrals glimmered with gold, sparkled with jewels. But not even in China did the poor seem so ragged, so ignorant, so filthy, and so despairing. Absalom was outraged when, in the churches, he saw wretched peasants worshipping relics of dead saints, pressing to their lips old and rotted bones, wisps of hair, fragments of dried skin.

"This can't last," Absalom said. "There'll be a revolution here within the next ten years—mark my words! People can't live like this and look like this without an explosion ahead."

The Sydenstrickers wandered about Europe visiting Poland, Germany, France, Switzerland, and England, with Absalom growing more glum each day and his opinion of the white race getting lower and lower, mainly because of the rudeness of the cab drivers and porters who complained about his very small tips. But Pearl, Grace, and Caroline drank in the sights and sounds of this ancient world, Caroline stressing to her children that Europe had given birth to America and one needed to understand one to appreciate the other. England in particular fascinated Pearl, for in the gentle loveliness of its land and in the courtesy and calm of its people she could find no clue at all to the arrogance and cruelty she had witnessed in many Englishmen serving in China.

They sailed for America. One night on board ship Pearl and her father had one of their rare talks. The uprising of the oppressed, which would begin in Russia, he said, would spread to the countries of Asia, where it would be directed against the white man.

"Americans, too?" Pearl wanted to know.

He replied, "The Chinese owe us nothing. We have done the best we could, but that, too, was our duty and so they still owe us nothing. And if our country has taken no concessions, we have kept silence when others did, and we too have profited from the unequal treaties. I don't think we shall escape when the day of reckoning comes."

And Pearl, eighteen, watched the ship's bow rise and fall, trembling toward America, and she felt a great sorrow for the whole troubled world.

They arrived in the United States in late summer of 1910 and Pearl was enrolled at Randolph-Macon Women's College in Lynchburg, Virginia. This was also the town where Edwin now lived. The college was new and the buildings, recently built, looked raw. It seemed strange to Pearl to be surrounded by such newness, for all her life she had been in ancient settings.

Absalom was invited to lead religious services in the college chapel, and Pearl, sitting with the other freshmen, squirmed in embarrassment as her father serenely moved to the lectern and began to speak in his dry, monotonous way. He wore a rusty old frock coat that was giving way at the seams and was outdated in style by many years. The girl sitting next to Pearl sighed and whispered in a soft Southern drawl, "He looks as though he'd be right long-winded."

"He's my father," Pearl admitted.

"Oh, I *am* sorry!"

"It doesn't matter," Pearl muttered bitterly. "He *is* long-winded!" And she sat there suffering while Absalom droned on without end.

Absalom, Caroline, and Grace visited the West Virginia home briefly before going back to China. It was not the same. Hermanus was dead and the house and its inhabitants were changed, full of their own lives. Caroline felt like a stranger. She had no role to play anymore in her native land. This time she went back to China willingly, and she felt sure that she would never see America again.

Pearl's classmates had no knowledge of the world from which she came, and to them what was different was suspect. Even more surprising to Pearl, they did not seem to have any curiosity about her world. She was anxious to talk, to exchange ideas, for she had thought a great deal about Asia and Europe and America, and she had had experience of them all. But these girls were not much interested in the world's affairs very far beyond the confines of Lynchburg, Virginia, and they were not at all interested in its agonies. What was there to talk about with these American girls who had lived such thin, protected lives? They used slang words whose meaning she did not even know, and sometimes she felt as if she had arrived from another planet.

She even looked different. Her dresses, copied from models in magazines and made with great skill and care by a Chinese tailor, who had used the finest Chinese silks and linen, were all the wrong length and in outdated styles. Her hair, she still wore in a thick braid doubled up and tied with a ribbon. Her handmade leather shoes, like her dresses, were dowdy in style even if lovingly fine in workmanship. Girls came in groups to stare at her, and as she passed among them on her way to classes she could hear their whispers and giggles.

There was a Chinese girl at Randolph-Macon, a senior, who stayed aloof from the others, isolated by her difference but apparently content to keep it that way. Pearl, too, sensed she was different and always would be, but she made up her mind to find a way of joining what she had been told was "her own kind."

And so she put away her Chinese-made clothes, pinned up her golden braids, and bought American dresses and shoes. She soon even managed to absorb a Virginia drawl. She copied the slang as if it were but another new language to learn, and she tried valiantly to find things to say about clothes and boys and sororities. By the end of the first year she had even managed to develop a real interest in some of those things, although as far as the boys were concerned those who were available were far too childish to make that interest more than talk.

In her disguise as an average American girl she was successful enough to get invited by college mates for visits to their homes. It amused her that their parents, learning of her background, were as lacking in curiosity as their daughters. If all America had the same indifferent attitude toward the rest of the world, she thought, it would go badly for America and the world.

As for her studies, she rapidly found that here as in Miss Jewell's school she would have to learn in her own way. For the first time in her life she was near a large library, and she read greedily, stealing hours from her assignments in Latin, math, and physics, all of which she detested. She had no need to study for such subjects as English and it took but a few classes for her English professor to realize that she could teach this girl nothing. The entire English class began to look forward to Pearl's composition exercises, for these were exciting little poems and narratives. The other subjects that absorbed her were philosophy and psychology—she came to these naturally, for her home background and all that was Asian in her loved above all things to ponder the origin and meaning of life and the way of one human being with another.

As the months passed, her classmates no longer thought her strange, but they knew she was not truly one of them. Yet the earlier suspicion had given way to admiration and some awe. They sensed she was a leader, wiser, more mature. And something drew them to her, perhaps the calm and patience that the East had bred into her, perhaps the bottomless blue eyes that seemed to know so much. They sought her out and confided in her. She listened, advised, and gave comfort.

But it bothered her then as it would for the rest of her life that she could never entirely return all they gave. She could not confide her innermost heart to anyone. In the midst of people, surrounded by love, she felt nevertheless alone.

She did not particularly like it that way. She was not fond of people who set themselves above others, and she did not admire this in herself. But she was more of the East than of the West, and all the ancient Eastern values so deeply rooted in her told her that one *accepted* and used the way things were, inside oneself as well as in the world. And that was the way it was. And, strangely, there was no haughtiness in it and others sensed that and it was why they came to her and would keep coming. At least some would, and others would resent it.

Thus, when she competed for the prize for the best short story and for the best poem of the year and won both top honors, there were some who felt unfairly treated. Yet, she was elected president of her junior class, and that represented for her the proof that she had become a full-fledged American.

Vacations were not happy for her during her college years. Her first summer vacation was partly spent at the home of her mother's family in West Virginia. Although she loved the beauty and cleanliness of the American countryside, she now found that she had even less in common with this small-town family of relatives than with her schoolmates. They were concerned mostly with small daily household matters and local affairs, and Pearl had become used to living and thinking on a world scale. But she learned to enjoy them, in her particular lonely way, simply by watching the impact of personalities, as if they were playing out a drama on a stage. And that was the way to endure almost anything, she learned, whether it was spending the time with this family or waiting for a train or suffering a boring meeting—one simply snapped the mind into a theater seat, became a spectator, and all the world became a stage.

It was harder to do that when vacation time brought her to her brother Edwin's house, for here she was deeply involved. Edwin lived in Lynchburg, in the same town as the college, and was editor of a newspaper there. A brilliant and cultivated man, he had married a woman too unlike him in her outlook and education, and now his home was being split apart by quarreling and unhappiness. Pearl loved her brother deeply and adored his two children, but staying in that house was a burden and such "vacations" shattered her. During her senior year she lived off-campus at her brother's house because he was away most of the time at a distant job and had asked that she keep watch over his children.

Discussing the matter with his sister, Edwin determined on a divorce and asked Pearl to write their parents. Caroline and Absalom's reply was so horrified, for they considered divorce a sin and one that had never occurred in the family history, that Edwin decided to postpone it. Yet he was unable to live with his wife and so he moved away and lived alone. Marriage could be difficult and delicate, Pearl learned, and she wondered if she would be able to avoid mistakes.

She read and wrote. A poem of hers, one of the several that appeared in the college paper, *The Tattler,* contained these lines of yearning:

> The light of evening stars gleams white,
> And now the nightingale's silver song
> Is weaving spells 'round the drowsy Earth:
> The twilight deepens again to night:
> > Night o'er the hills of Tang—
> > Night o'er the heart of me!
> And hopeless shadows are stealing long
> And silent over the distant lea;
> O, heart of mine, though the stars shine on,
> What matters it when the sun is gone?

The college years sped. In the spring of 1914 she walked down the line of graduates to receive her diploma and carry it in triumph to her brother Edwin, who was in the audience.

Which of her two worlds, America or China, would claim her now? Her conscience moved her to return to China and join her parents in missionary work. Yet her instincts repelled that notion. She hated the idea of attempting to persuade anyone to change his religion and she had long ago rejected the idea that her religion was superior to any other. She recognized, too, that much brutality and oppression hid under the cloak of religion and she did not want to be a part of that. But China called.

America, her other world, called more strongly. She had come to love it and felt keenly that she knew only a small part of this land. Beyond the college walls was a vast and varied country she longed to see, for it was truly hers. She was in fact an American now. College had done that much for her, and perhaps much more than she was willing to recognize. Most tempting of all, she could take her pick of several teaching jobs that had been offered her, including one to remain on at the college as an instructor in psychology, and that is what she did for a few months.

Then came a letter from Absalom, telling her that Caroline was ill with a disease called tropical sprue. This disease so affected the digestive system that most food could not be absorbed. Its victims commonly wasted away from anemia and malnutrition. Today there is effective treatment for the disease, but at that time little was known about treating it. Pearl packed her bags and wrote to the Presbyterian Board of Missions to ask that she be sent back to China as a teacher.

On the ship across the Pacific Ocean she discovered that she was beginning to think in Chinese again, after four years. As for her second language, she was surprised to find how she had drifted into a Southern drawl—a young man aboard ship, Philip by name, who also introduced her to the fine and ancient art of kissing, laughed at her accent and even corrected her pronunciation of the word *China,* which she intoned as "Chahna."

And then there was land on the western horizon and the

blue Pacific turned yellow where the Yangtze River, draining half a continent, poured into it. And all the sandalwood smells of the Orient embraced the ship as it slid into a harbor crisscrossed by slat-sailed junks. And she was home. And "Chahna" was China again.

Six

And Love—Perhaps

The big ship anchored offshore in the Yangtze River, for the water near the Shanghai wharves was too shallow for it. From the rail Pearl could see the little tender puffing out to meet the ship, and eagerly she scanned the figures on board. It was not too hard to pick out Absalom, by far the tallest, but where was Caroline? The scrawny little figure beside Absalom was not Caroline but Grace. Pearl's heart sank.

As the tender neared and Absalom came aboard and prowled among the passengers, passing his daughter many times, Pearl finally realized that her father did not recognize her. He had always been shy of staring too intently at any woman, even in search of his own daughter.

"Father!" she said at last and took his arm.

"Well, of course," Absalom mumbled, taking a sharper look from the corner of his eye. "But I didn't know what to look for!"

Caroline had not been strong enough even to make the train journey to Shanghai, Absalom confirmed. But she was waiting at the railroad station in Chinkiang at the head of a cheering delegation of neighbors and friends. She was painfully thin, shrunken to half her size, it seemed. Pearl, embracing her mother, lifted her into the air. "Mother, how little you are!"

"Daughter, how big you are!" Caroline laughed.

Then came the greetings from friends carrying their tributes of sesame cookies and sponge cakes. They walked home in procession, past earthen houses and fields where farmers and their wives laid aside their hoes and came down to the road to shout, "And have you come back? It is good—it is good."

And then she was home, a new house because the old compound had been turned into a school for boys, but Caroline's touch was there in the bedroom that had been set aside for Pearl, in the starched white curtains and the inevitable fresh roses on the table. At last the guests were gone and she could embrace the frail bird that her mother had become and she could learn how the disease had laid waste to Caroline's strong body and lined her mouth with sores so painful that frequently she could not speak, much less eat. But now that Pearl was back, Caroline declared brightly, she would put up even a stronger fight against the illness.

No other task seemed half as important to Pearl as joining this battle and winning it. She set about learning as much about the disease as she could. In trying to find some course of treatment that would help, she and Caroline wrote to everyone they could find who had suffered from the disease. "No use asking about the dead ones," Caroline advised, laughing.

Some of the letters that came back reported that special diets seemed helpful. Thus, for several months Pearl fed her mother bananas, which Caroline hated, but the fruit seemed to do no good. Then, for a while, it was strawberries, and when this brought no abatement of Caroline's suffering, they turned to fresh raw cow's milk. This was a major problem, for it was not part of the general Chinese diet. When at last they located a cow, it became a match of Pearl's wits against those of the farmer to make sure that the milk was not watered.

One night Caroline's strength wavered, almost flickered out. "Child, is this d-e-a-t-h?" she whispered, spelling the dread word.

"I will not let you die!" Pearl cried. She held her mother's hand tightly and tried to will her own strength into those pitiful limbs.

Caroline did not die then, but regained enough strength for Pearl to take her up to Kuling, in the beautiful mountains of Lu where the Sydenstrickers, like many other white families, had built a house as a summer escape from the dank plague-ridden air of the valley. Gently Pearl guided her mother aboard the little English steamer that puffed up the river to Kinkiang. Here they climbed into sedan chairs and were borne, with their baggage, on the shoulders of porters up narrow trails along cliffs falling hundreds of feet. At last they were in the little stone house, where the air was crisp and cool, brooks ran clear, and wild fern and lilies grew. Absalom, who had found the place, had said it was like the Allegheny Mountains back home.

For a year Pearl stayed with her mother and nursed her. Carefully she tried various combinations of foods, seeking those to which Caroline would respond. For one period Caroline valiantly fed on an odious mixture of boiled liver and spinach. Slowly she improved, and it began to look as if the battle was being won. While her mother rested, Pearl read Chinese books, exploring the long history of the Chinese novel.

She went for solitary walks along the hillsides and wondered what life held for her.

In her heart she had always known she would write. Stories crept into her mind unbidden, demanding to be told. The people she had known, faces she had seen, sometimes only for a blindingly sharp but brief moment, in a field, in a hut, on a boat, jostled in her head like prisoners demanding to be freed. Language rang in her ears like music, but it was formless yet, not her own sound, sometimes ornate with the curlicues of Chinese, sometimes round and swelling with the tumult of the Bible, sometimes stately with the march of the English poets.

She knew she was not yet ready to write. The things that filled her head did not yet belong to her; she had seen them but she had not lived them. And she knew, moreover, that they were drawn from a circle of experience far too narrow. She felt empty. She needed a point of view, a whole way of looking at life that was her own.

Many years later she would say, "I know now, of course, that emptiness is the normal state of youth. No writer, I believe, should attempt a novel before he is thirty, and not then unless he has been hopelessly and helplessly involved in life. For the writer who goes out to find material for a novel, as a fisherman goes out to sea to fish, will certainly not write a good novel. Life has to be lived thoughtlessly, unconsciously, at full tilt and for no purpose except its own sake before it becomes, eventually, good material for a novel."

And this was what she longed for, not "material" but more of life. She felt desperately isolated while all around her, it seemed, the very earth shook. In Europe a war raged, involving most of the Western nations, and all she knew about it came from brief reports in an English paper that reached Kuling from time to time. In China, great changes had come about and she had not, since her return, had much chance to absorb them.

For the old Chinese Empire of the Manchus was no more. While she was in college, revolutionary forces had overthrown the wasteful and corrupt old regime of the Empress Dowager. They had hunted down and slaughtered the hated Manchu aristocracy. In pity Caroline had hidden dainty Manchu ladies and their children, fleeing for their lives. The queue, the long thin braid worn by men, was seized on as a symbol of the years of backwardness imposed by the Manchus, and the soldiers of the revolution sliced them off the scalps of rich men and peasants alike.

Dr. Sun Yat-sen, a leader who had abandoned his profession as physician, then attempted to bring about a new China that could take its place among modern nations. A Christian who had traveled in America and Europe, Sun Yat-sen tried to unite the Chinese around the goal of creating a republic, a constitutional form of government like that of the United States, with himself as president.

It was a difficult task. Eighty-five percent of the Chinese people were peasants who could not read or write. They neither knew nor cared what went on beyond the confines of the villages, where they toiled then as always for the bare necessities of life. They knew nothing of democracy, and one type of ruler seemed to them as good or as bad as the other, nor did it matter to whom taxes were paid. At least the old Empress Dowager had sometimes brought some pomp and drama into their lives.

And if the centuries-old suspicion of the people were not

enough of an obstacle, Sun Yat-sen faced the power of the warlords who tore China into pieces. The warlords, most of whom answered to the title of general, ruled over parcels of China, and each considered his territory his private preserve. A warlord collected taxes, maintained a private army, and had power of life and death over the people. Somehow the powerful warlords would have to be abolished before Sun Yat-sen could achieve his goal.

As for the educated classes, they were hopelessly divided. On his side Sun Yat-sen could count those who knew that the modernization of China depended on educating its people, so that industries could be developed and a government by representation be established. But they did not know how to move the people. Their own lives were out of touch with peasant China.

There were others—classical scholars and gentlefolk—who mistrusted the coarse peasants and hated the idea of democracy. Some, while applauding the downfall of the Manchurian overlords who had ruled captive China for so many centuries, only wished for a Chinese emperor instead and that the old ways be retained. Then there were others who saw the unsettled times as an opportunity for their own ambitions. Conflict raged, too, between the young and the old, between those trained in Western ways in the missionary schools, such as those run by Pearl's father, and those new radicals who declared that the foreign churches and their interference would always hold China back.

This was an exciting time to be in China and Pearl yearned to be in the middle of it. The political turmoil was reflected in a great ferment in literature and the arts, and that was where her heart lay.

At last, one day in winter, when Caroline was well enough to manage her own recovery, Pearl left her mother in the care of friends, walked down the mountain to the river, and took the boat to Chinkiang. For the time being, she had set death back on its heels, and now she was ready for life.

At the mission house she kept house for her father, taught at a missionary school for Chinese boys, and buried herself in the reading of Chinese literature and the attempt to understand what was happening in China. Her teaching was pure joy, because the families from whom her students came had a reverence for education. Her young charges soaked up everything she could teach them and eagerly came back for more. There was none of the boredom or the frustration of trying to cram learning into unwilling minds that was so much a part of American schools, even of the college she had attended. Pearl's students stimulated her, and she could see that the brightest ones, taking what they needed from school, would reject the religious part. The best Chinese minds, she knew, would not turn to the service of Christianity but to that of China. They would break free.

She longed to break free herself. The rules of the missionary school were strict. The narrow religion taught by the missions and the tight codes of conduct they insisted on hardly gave her room to breathe. She lived bounded by little minds and little morals. When she tried to break out of the circle by accepting dates with some of the young men who were employed by British or American tobacco and oil companies, the older missionary women clucked their disapproval. They told her that if she went with the godless and irreverent business people she would have to leave the missionary circle.

"I am not a missionary," she protested. "I am a teacher!"

But that did not make any difference. As long as she taught in a missionary school, her behavior must cause no ripple of criticism. She could not live in two worlds, they said. That was ridiculous to her, for she felt a full person should live in many worlds. Although her parents gave her freedom, to ease the pressure on them she gave up her few friends in the business community.

She was desperately lonely. There were no interesting or attractive young men in the missionary settlement, nor young women either, for that matter. The American woman closest to her in years was of a different generation at age thirty-five, wife of a missionary, and mother of three children. The Chinese girls with whom she had grown up were busy with their own children and households, all of them married in the traditional Chinese way according to arrangements made by their parents. They worried that Pearl's parents seemed to be doing nothing about arranging a marriage for her, and they began to put pressure on them.

Caroline, American to the end, sniffed angrily at the idea. But Absalom, who had become more Chinese than American, actually tried to arrange to marry off Pearl to a Chinese man of well-placed family. Pearl, partly amused, partly angry (even though the young man in question was both handsome and brilliant), nevertheless held her tongue because she knew the family and was sure they would never agree for the son to marry a white woman.

Then, all at once, she fell in love—perhaps.

John Lossing Buck was a young American agriculturist, newly arrived in China. Not a missionary himself, he was employed by the Presbyterian Mission Board to teach modern farming methods to the Chinese. He was tall, ruddy, very handsome and strong. His manner was modest and simple. He seemed like a good man.

He was not an intellectual. He did not love books; he was a stranger to poetry; strong responses to beauty either puzzled or embarrassed him. But perhaps those things would come, Pearl felt. After all, did not people grow? True, he did not seem to have many ideas of his own, but then perhaps that was because he was shy and needed to learn better ways of putting ideas into language.

Anyway, people should not be alike, she reasoned. It was important to have respect—even love—for differences. John was a strong, practical man, and he had a winning smile.

Was it that smile, the broad chest, the long straight legs? Was it some kind of magic that no one could explain? Love as a wild and uncontrollable passion was something she had read about but had never seen. Her own parents surely gave no example of it, yet they worked together and lived lives of meaning, if sometimes sadness. None of her Chinese friends had married for love, yet love had come to many, and when it did, Pearl observed, it rooted itself solidly in people who had knowledge of each other. In the Asian way of thinking—and in this Pearl was more Asian than Western—marriage was part of life's round, necessary for the body's yearning and for the solemn obligation to continue the chain of family.

A feeling for the rhythms of life was strong in Pearl. This was the right time for marriage. She felt that *she needed the experience of marriage.* And she needed to break out of the little mission community; she wanted a way to set foot on the path of her own life.

All these things, in the year 1917, spelled love for Pearl. Very few people have ever satisfactorily defined love, and then only for themselves. Whatever it was, it fastened itself on John Buck, and she decided to marry him after having only seen him some four times under the watchful eyes of chaperones.

The strongest objection to her plans came from Caroline and Absalom. They were frank. John would not fit into the bookish Sydenstricker family, they said. But it was mainly Pearl's happiness that concerned them. Pearl could never be found without a book or John with one. "We know you better than you can imagine, and how can you be happy unless you live with someone who understands what you are talking about?"

But Pearl had made up her mind. Of course, her parents would resist, for marriage to John Buck would mean that she would move far away into the northern part of China where his assignment was. Marriage would make possible the break-away that was so difficult before.

Pearl and John Buck were married in a simple ceremony, and very soon after, they traveled north to the far province of Anwei, where they settled into a little Chinese house in the ancient walled town of Nanhsüchou.

Seven

※

Life, Death, and Writing

No longer could she see blue hills and fertile green valleys; here in Nanhsüchou the buff-colored land stretched flat. The land lay naked in winter, but in spring it came alive with fruit-tree blossoms, and soon after that wheat and ferny willows billowed in the incessant wind. Under the summer sun frequent mirages shimmered in the haze, and then the eye was tricked into seeing fairy lakes and hills.

The Bucks' house hugged the shadow of the town wall. A wide moat surrounded the wall. At night the huge gates clanged shut against bandits and wandering soldiers. And then Pearl could walk the dusty unpaved streets lit only by moonlight, and she could peer into the open doors of shops and houses where families gathered around their suppers and the light of a candle or bean oil lamp. The wall joined them, gathered them under its wing. Pearl had a sense of being closer to the Chinese people than ever before.

She busied herself with her home, a little four-room house of gray brick with a black tile roof. This was the first house over which she had full charge, and she discovered what would become a lifelong delight in surrounding herself with an orderly and harmonious environment. She painted walls and then painted pictures to hang on them, sewed yellow silk curtains for the windows, designed bookshelves, arranged furniture and straw mats, and grew a garden for the flowers that, to her as to her mother, were so important a part of every home.

When Caroline and Grace came to visit, they found the house a deeply restful place, the colors subdued—blacks and tans and gold, with splashes of color from flowers and cushions —and the open fire merrily at work and, as Grace later reported, "meals served up with the art of a French chef."

If she had sought freedom through marriage, she found it, but not as she expected. Before long she realized that Absalom and Caroline had been right. It took a very short time for Pearl and John to exhaust the little they had in common. Where Pearl's imagination, feeling, and interest went soaring, John could not follow. She had "a man around the house"— as she put it—but no real companion for the long trails her mind needed to pursue. There were long silent evenings with absolutely nothing to talk about, with no way of reaching one another.

What to do about it? Pearl's missionary training and her Asian upbringing allowed for little to do but accept it and build a life around it. Divorce was out of the question, even if the thought occurred to her. It probably didn't. She was married; she had a home; she would have her work in the world as John had his; she would have many children; and these were the conditions of life that one arranged and built on. Indeed, when she thought about it, marriage had changed little in her life—she was still alone, an observer seeing things others did not, knowing what they did not, with no one near who could follow her. The sense of apartness, which she had tried to end, had not ended.

Like an Asian woman, she hid this insight completely from her husband, never once hinting where he failed her, never doing anything that would slight his manhood. John Buck had no occasion to believe that his marriage was not a success. His wife always was there when he needed her; she accomplished all a wife was supposed to, seemed agreeable, and kept a generally calm house. True, she maintained a bewildering schedule of activity and had her head buried in a book the rest of the time, and true, there were those fantastic ideas that he could not follow about religion and art and literature, and true, there were those occasional explosions of temper that went as quickly as they came—but none of it really interfered with the order of things a man needed around him.

Now a married woman, Pearl could move about the town and countryside with less fear of breaking the rules of proper behavior. The people were friendly and curious, and seeing that Pearl was so accessible and spoke Chinese as fluently as they themselves, they heaped on her invitations to weddings, feasts, and family affairs. Her own door was always open, and an endless stream of visitors made use of it. They came for friendship, for advice, and because of the rare quality that led people of all ages and all backgrounds to come and lay their lives in her lap.

The currents of Chinese life swirled around her. There was the loving wife who hung herself when her husband brought home a young concubine. There was proud Madame Wu, aristocratic and brilliant, tottering on bound feet just three inches long, ruling her household with ruthless authority, yet curious about the ways and ideas of the West. What a subject for a book she would make! There was jolly Madame Chang to furnish her own soft shoulder when Pearl's heart ached. The rights of sons, the obligations of daughters, the matters of inheritance and family loyalty—all these timeless matters were now being played out under great conflict because of the revolutionary new ideas that had reached the young people of even this far corner of China. Some young women desired education and more freedom for themselves, and some young men, sent away to school, decided they did not want to return home but rather wished to find an independent life for themselves in the service of China.

Taking over a school for young girls plunged Pearl even more deeply into the life of the town and the hearts of its young people. An American doctor in the town, his own wife so appalled by China that she never left the house, called frequently on Pearl to act as his nurse. She helped at childbirths and comforted families faced with death, and this activity, too, pulled her into the raw exposed substance of living. Sometimes, outside the locked gates of the town, conflicts raged between warlords, bullets cracked over the town walls, and then she helped minister to the wounds of the soldiers.

John needed to travel the countryside in his work as an agriculturist, and Pearl often went with him as translator, for his command of Chinese was weak. Beyond the walls of the town lay the entirely different world of the Chinese peasant. As much of the earth as weed, the peasants lived with the march of the seasons and the turn of the planet, locked in battle with the soil for each grain of wheat and each bean. The peasants were uneducated in the ways of books and pencils, but Pearl saw that their knowledge, accumulated through centuries, was vast in other things—in their understanding of the land, in their tolerance of each other, in their sense of their own dignity, and in their bottomless capacity to keep on struggling in the face of extraordinary hardship and disappointment.

The only means proper for a woman to travel the countryside was by sedan chair, and thus Pearl went sailing along on the shoulders of trotting and seemingly tireless bearers, with John sedately bicycling alongside. While John dealt with the farmers, she spent her time with the women and children. They were intensely curious about her, aghast that she spoke so freely to her husband and did not bow before him as was their own custom. She learned about their lives and was deeply moved by their utter lack of selfishness, the incredible lengths of pain and hardship they endured to serve their men and families. There was material here for many stories that could trace this close compact of man, woman, child, and earth.

Of these farmer folk she said, "They were the ones who bore the brunt of life, who made the least money and did the most work. They were the most real, the closest to the earth, to birth and death, to laughter and to weeping. To visit the farm families became my own search for reality, and among them I found the human being as he most nearly is."

Frequently John's negotiations with the farmers broke down for want of language, and then in desperation Pearl was summoned to serve as translator. These discussions gave her insight into the world of the peasant man, his habit of thought, and the ways in which he scratched his livelihood from the ground.

She began to realize that her husband was in trouble. The farming methods used by the peasants were far from primitive. Their ancestors had tilled the same soil for thousands of years with methods evolved out of experience, tenacity, and great cleverness. On farms rarely larger than five acres they were able to produce from the scraggly earth enough to keep large families in simple comfort. Against frequent drought, high dry winds, and long cold winters they achieved agricultural miracles unmatched by American farmers, who would most likely abandon such terrain and climate to the coyotes before attempting to plant it. It was evident to her that these farmers had more to tell John than he had to teach them. She kept her doubts to herself, however. Asian women simply did not contradict their men—and the reason was not so much fear as fineness of feeling.

Pearl and John traveled to remote towns where no Westerner had ever been. Here, behind the town walls the round of life went on as it had for centuries, and relationships among people were developed to a high art. Every detail of manner and behavior between husband and wife, wife and concubine, parent and child, daughter and mother-in-law, was prescribed by thousands of years of tradition, like some formal ballet— and yet within this dance Pearl could perceive the little meaningful variations brought about by pride, power, brilliance, generosity, and meanness. Here and there special men and women stood out like peaks, and their force of intelligence and character would have made them memorable in any time, in any land.

One day they would all find their way into stories she would write. But when? It seemed she was filled to bursting with the need to write, and also with the fear of writing, but that had not yet happened which could break the ring of restraint. Perhaps she had not yet completely settled in her mind how far to go along with the decision to live in her own way. If she wrote and her writing were accepted, the distance between her and John, already large, would not only become larger but more visible to all the world. He would be hurt. It was not the Asian way to do this to a man. Everything in her training held her back from this commitment of herself from which there was no return; but everything that was truly herself told her to put pen to paper and let happen what might, to follow her sympathy.

The three years in Nanhsüchou ended when John, sensing that he was floundering, applied for and secured a job teaching agriculture at the University of Nanking. They moved south to that city, once capital of the Chinese Empire in days of the Ming dynasty, before the Manchus.

A walled city set among lovely mountains and valleys, Nanking and its surroundings furnished a feast for the eye, especially to one fresh from the bleak plateaus of the north. Here could be found mountainsides carpeted with flowers, shaggy with trees. Nestled in the hills were fine old temples and ancient tombs. Pearl, wandering about these, sat in their shade, wondering about herself and wondering, too, about the baby she now knew she carried. Even the wide walls of the city were lovely, set in brick. Unlike most walled cities, Nanking was planned for space enough to contain trees, gardens, ponds. From the attic room of her Nanking house she could see Purple Mountain, the city wall, a pagoda, her garden, and a bamboo grove.

It was only a two-hour train journey to Chinkiang, so Pearl was able to visit her parents often and share with Caroline the fun of waiting for the baby to come. In March 1921, Carol was born, round and strong and healthy; or so it seemed. Uplifted with joy, Pearl plunged into the rituals of motherhood, and the idea of writing did not burn so fiercely in her mind. She could never have enough of babies, she determined. She would have a large family, a busy house. Carol seemed so amiable and pleasant an infant. But sometimes a passing shadow of fear stopped Pearl's heart. Was her baby's quietness merely content or was it something else?

Another shadow darkened her happiness. It soon became apparent that she was not recovering well from childbirth, that something was radically wrong. In search of expert medical care she made a quiet, brief journey to America, her baby in a basket on her arm. There she left Carol with Grace, who was attending an American college, and entered a hospital. When she came out a couple of weeks later, after an operation, it was with the bitter knowledge that she would never bear another child. Well, she would love this one child enough for ten, and perhaps sometime later she would find another way to fill her house with children. The journey back to China was grim.

That was a dark year, for back in China she found Caroline sinking rapidly. As death neared and as she recognized it, Caroline would have nothing to do with Absalom; she scarcely permitted him into the sickroom. Stubbornly she clung to life, determined to live at least until Grace returned from America. It became necessary to hire a nurse, who turned out to be a ruin of a woman, with bleached hair and a painted mask of a face, whose life had been lived in the honky-tonk alleys of Shanghai and Hong Kong. Immediately Caroline had the woman's entire life story, and she soothed, "I know— I know how hard it is to be good—especially when no answer comes and one goes on waiting in the dark."

One day Pearl entered the bedroom and was greeted by the blaring sound of jazz music played on a scratchy Victrola. The nurse, cheeks puffing with effort, was dancing about the room, and Caroline was watching in delight. The patient had asked for a demonstration of a fox-trot, the latest American dance craze, which she had read about but had never seen.

Grace came, finally, just before Caroline's strength gave out. One grim October afternoon the nurse hurried from the sickroom to tell them Caroline was breathing her last. Pearl could not bring herself to enter the bedroom, but stayed outside in the hall staring out the window at a landscape drowned in tears, while Absalom and Grace went in. In a little while Absalom came out. "She's gone," he said, strangely calm, and then he turned and plodded to his study to be alone with his life and his God. They buried her the next day in the little walled cemetery, near Clyde's grave.

Back home in Nanking, Pearl wondered how she could ever fill this chasm in her life. The attic room beckoned her, a corner all her own. She began to spend more and more time up there. That year, with its changes and disappointments and pain, had shaken her severely. Until now, she had observed the tragedies of others, but now she was on deeply personal terms with pain.

She began setting down Caroline's story. Now that the story had ended she could see it whole, as if from a distance, even as she could view Tze-ch'ing Shan, Nanking's Purple Mountain, looming out her window past the bowl of bright flowers. The story demanded to be told and would not wait.

And this was like giving birth again, to coax words and paragraphs and pages into life, to master and re-create the truth. Caroline lived once more as a young girl ripe with yearning, seeking some task and purpose on which to fasten her overflowing energy. Hesitating between what would employ her sense of fun and what would command her young passion for service, she settled at last on the grim duties offered by Absalom. And for the rest of her life she was torn between fun and duty, the light and song in her fighting the joyless call of a missionary's god. Duty and Absalom told her that a person's proper concern was for man's soul and his relationship with God, but every instinct that bubbled through told her that the finest concern of man was with mankind and his relationship with other human beings.

In the gathering pile of papers Caroline loved her children again, wept over their graves, sang at her organ, tended her beloved roses, sparkled with fun and laughter and mischief, worried about her sins, gathered her friends, battled the corrupt, scorned the bigoted, tweaked Absalom's coattails when he got too long-winded, fought her husband for pennies for children's comforts, and yearned for her lost America.

It was a life lived for others, heeding calls that came from outside. What would that life have been had Caroline followed her heart? The question was very much alive for Pearl, still struggling with what her own heart told her to do. How did one find the balance between one's duty to others and to oneself—and, in the end, was there truly a difference? When she had come upon the nurse skittering around Caroline's sickroom in a fox-trot, she had heard her mother say wistfully, now close to death, "Well, that's a pretty thing—so graceful and light. I should not be surprised if Absalom is all wrong about God. I believe one ought to choose the happy, bright things of life, like dancing and laughter and beauty. I think if I had to do it all over again, I would choose these instead of thinking them sinful. Who knows?—God might like them."

And then, inevitably, as Caroline lived again in the manuscript, so again she died, and the story was told. Now what should be done with it? The truth was in that pile of papers, but the truth would hurt, for Absalom was yet alive and would be so for many years, and Pearl had not spared him in the telling. Then again, this was the first book she had written, and she was not indeed certain that it was a book or that anyone would want to read it. She was sure only of its truth and that she had written the book for her child, so that when Carol was old enough to read she could meet her grandmother in its pages. The book had so much become Caroline herself that at the time it almost seemed a sacrilege to send it out among strangers. She packed it carefully, sealed it in a box, and hid it high in a wall closet.

But the deed had been done. She had written a book, whether anyone knew it or not. She had breathed life into dead pages. She had struggled with words, created sentences, destroyed them, refined them, fitted them into a design of meaning, puzzled over what was really true and what merely seemed true. And when the book was finished, her creation whole, she felt lost without it. The desk was empty and it beckoned for more.

Pearl Buck had become a writer.

Caroline, who had put her daughter on so many paths, had given one last hearty shove.

Eight

༺ஓ༒

Writer and Everything Else

She was a writer now, but she was also a daughter, mother, housewife, and teacher.

She taught English and American literature at the University of Nanking. In her classes new and old ideas clashed, East and West mingled. Young Chinese writers were rediscovering the art of storytelling and the colorful language of the people from the street storytellers. They were taking American and English novelists as their models. Every discussion about English literature became linked to what was happening in China. The students shared with their teacher their groping, their enthusiasms, and their family problems.

Three American writers—Theodore Dreiser, Ellen Glasgow, and Sinclair Lewis—particularly moved Pearl and she sought to make her students understand what these authors were doing. They reached beyond the polite and artificial themes of the past and sought to reflect what was real in American life, even when it hurt. She envied these writers for something she would never have—their intense American experience. Would she herself, now thirty years old, ever be able to write so penetratingly about American people and life? They had lived it; its consciousness had been hammered into them during their growing years; but her American world came mostly from books, her mother's tales, and a brief college sojourn.

She was a wife, too. John was floundering no less in the university than in the fields around Nanhsüchou. There was something obviously wrong about trying to teach American agriculture, from American textbooks, to Chinese. The land was different, as was its ownership and as were the tools. Moreover, the northern China experience had shown her and John that the Chinese had developed superior methods of their own, especially suited to their own conditions.

John needed help in getting set on the right track, and Pearl's creative mind found the way. But gently, gently—the Asian style of influencing people was to plant ideas in such a way that the person to be persuaded believed they were his own. The precious margin of a man's pride must be maintained at all costs. This was the delicate art of human relations she had learned so well from Madame Wu and the families of Nanhsüchou.

Led by Pearl's subtle questions and suggestions, John began to see that a Chinese university needed not a science of American agriculture but one of Chinese agriculture, which had never yet been assembled into a discipline. Not only would this spread knowledge of Chinese methods through China but also through the rest of the world. There were more than enough experts on Western methods—why not become an authority on Chinese farming? The first thing to do was to gather the facts and organize them into a text, thus creating a body of knowledge that could be taught.

Why not use the students themselves to gather this information, sending them into the countryside with questionnaires? This would be a good practical learning experience for them, and best of all, and dearest to Pearl's motives, it might help close the gap between town and country and blunt the scorn most Chinese intellectuals felt for laboring folks.

The project took shape, and soon John was happily on his way toward becoming a major authority on Chinese farm life. The first small book resulting from this, most of it written by Pearl, was published by the University of Chicago and became a basic text for farm students and those interested in Asian affairs.

Well, she was a daughter, too. Absalom, now seventy, was at the end of his rope. Here, too, delicate means would have to be employed against what was most surely one of the most stubborn, proud, and least persuadable of men. His insistence on doing things his own way had by this time roused a storm of opposition in the missionary movement. The opposition objected because he had tried to establish a native church, led by Chinese instead of foreign preachers.

Up to then, he had sniffed at the opposition, dismissing them as carping, bigoted, narrow-visioned men, and he had cheerfully gone his own way. He would have denied it, but Caroline's support had given him more strength and independence than he knew. Now Caroline was gone and in her place was Grace, fresh from college, desperate with loneliness, and overwhelmed by the task of coping with this embattled old man.

The opposition came with proof of corruption in the churches he had established and with papers of resignation for him to sign. Absalom, never a judge of character, could not see that many of those whose souls he believed he had saved were rascals who were using him and the church as a source of money and influence. Confused now, he wavered between fight and surrender. The opposition went out into the villages to close down his churches. He mounted his ancient horse, as gaunt and bony and white as he himself, and rode out into the countryside to reestablish them, only to find his precious "Christians" gone. Absalom Sydenstricker had lost his way and needed help.

Pearl worked out a plan. She went to the seminary at Nanking, which Absalom himself had helped found, and begged that her father be given a job teaching young clergymen. The director was cold to the idea. He knew Absalom and had more than once experienced his stubbornness and wrath. There were no vacancies, he said, and besides, younger men were needed. But he reckoned without Caroline's daughter. Pearl pointed out that this was China, where old people were valued for their wisdom. She came back time and time again, storming the director's office with fresh arguments, until the man cringed at the sight of her.

In a moment of weakness he mused, "Of course we have planned a sort of correspondence school . . ."

"The very thing!" cried Pearl, adding craftily, "It wouldn't cost you anything—his salary from home would go on."

Before the director knew what was happening, the project was under way. Pearl made sure that the letter of invitation was an enthusiastic one and that it included a tempting title— Dean of the Correspondence School. She flew ahead of the letter and managed to be with Absalom when it arrived. The correspondence school did not yet exist, and it would be exciting for him to set up something entirely new and his own, she pointed out. He could come to live with her in Nanking and run his independent churches from there without interference, and there would also be time for him to work on his lifelong project of translating the Old Testament. It meant freedom and useful work, she tempted.

Absalom took the bait. It seemed like God's will, he said. Pearl assured him that such most certainly appeared to be the case.

So Absalom went to live with Pearl, scorning the large room she set aside for him and choosing a smaller one stripped of curtains and frills. He met with student clergymen, who stimulated him. He adored teaching. He set about with enormous energy to plan the correspondence school and here at last found a use for his own translation of the Bible, which he made a basic text. The old fire still moving him, he would stop on his way home from the seminary to preach the Word of the Lord on street corners, and to give away to ricksha coolies the vests and scarves and coats that Pearl vainly tried to make him wear. He was blissfully happy and he would be so for his remaining ten years of life.

For Pearl those years brought new understanding. Once she had feared her father and there had been times when she had even hated him, had been exasperated by him, and had resented his unbending will. But she enjoyed Absalom now and saw him with love. Spending the evening hours talking to him, she found depths of wit and gaiety in him that she had not known were there. On scholarly subjects his range of knowledge was as vast as his understanding of people was tiny. He was a thoroughly happy man whose contentment lay not in material things but in spending himself. She found it easier now, and indeed irresistible, to lavish affection on him, and she discovered, with some surprise, that underneath his gruffness he liked and needed it.

And she was a writer. Ideas for stories and novels piled

up on the attic desk, but she put off developing these for a time. She would first try her hand at more modest things. She wrote a small essay, light in feeling, which she entitled "In China, Too." In it she told how new trends were appearing among the young people of China, and she contrasted these with the more radical youth trends reported by newspapers in England and America—the shortened skirts, smoking, dancing. She did this with humor, describing the activity in a Chinese city street going on as it had for centuries, the young timid before their elders, the maidens locked behind curtains and walls. And then she noted how some young people were questioning the old ways, wearing Western clothes, becoming more defiant of their parents. While she mourned the passing of courtesy and gentle tradition, she noted that it was time for change, for clear thinking, and for an end to ignorance—"to the winds, then, with my slow, conservative soul and love of old-time reverence and manners!"

She typed the essay as well as she could, which was badly, and sent it off to an American magazine, the *Atlantic Monthly*. To her great joy, the most important moment in a writer's life came soon after—the first letter of acceptance from a publisher.

The editor of *Forum,* another American magazine, saw her article and wrote to ask if she could write one for him. She wrote another essay called "Beauty in China," which was published in that magazine. She told how so much of China's beauty in its land and handicrafts lay hidden under the pall of overcrowding and poverty, ignored by laborers too overwhelmed by the mere struggle for bread, or forgotten by idle folk impressed by Western things. Yet here and there wizened old women nursed a pot of flowers and the wild children of the streets begged for posies. "No," she concluded, "the love of beauty waits to be born in the heart of every child, I think. Sometimes the hard exigencies of life kill it, and it is still forever. But sometimes it lives and grows strong in the silent, meditative soul of a man or a woman, who finds that it is not enough to live in a palace and to dine even with kings."

Yet another article, "The Chinese Student Mind," was accepted by *The Nation*. She had tried her wings and was now aloft, flying on her own, but not yet anywhere near the heights beckoned by her true love, the novel.

If her writing gave her hope, motherhood brought despair. It was obvious that something was radically wrong with Carol. Although the child was strong and healthy in body, her mind seemed stunted. She could not be taught to speak or to respond to anything but the most simple kind of direction. She easily became nervous and cranky. Pearl felt she needed to confer with specialists who were not available in China.

John was eligible for a year's sabbatical leave in 1925, when Carol was four, and they decided to spend it in the United States. There they could get expert medical advice while John continued his studies at Cornell University. She, too, would enter the university to study for a master's degree in the English novel and essay.

On the ship to America she had many hours to herself while the child slept. Long conversations with John had never been possible, and by now she was indifferent to his presence. To fill her loneliness she found a corner in the dining saloon, and there in a notebook she wrote her first story. Drawn from real characters, its theme was the one that fascinated her the most, the upheaval in China caused by the conflict between old and new, between East and West, as it affected the lives of young people.

She told the story in the form of a letter written by Kwei-lan, a young woman deeply disturbed by her marriage. According to ancient custom, the marriage had been arranged by both sets of parents when bride and groom were children. Kwei-lan, raised in the old way, her feet bound to make them tiny, reveres her parents and believes herself inferior to men and but her husband's servant. On her bridal night her husband, trained as a physician and determined to practice medicine even though wealthy and able to live in idleness, turns her world upside down by informing her bluntly that he expects her to be not his obedient slave but an equal and a companion. She must unbind her deformed feet, live with him in their own house instead of with his parents, and bend her head to no one, not even to his own mother. Further, she must educate herself in the new ways and become a modern woman.

Kwei-lan, terrified by this challenge, cannot come out of the ivory shell in which she has lived her life so far. As a result, her husband is cool to her. In a way, the old customs help win out, because when Kwei-lan tells her astounded mother about her problem, the mother tells her that as a proper Chinese wife she has no choice but to obey her husband in all things. She unbinds her feet, begins to study modern ideas, learns about science, and finally gains her husband's admiration and affection.

Pearl finished the story before the boat docked at Vancouver. Rereading it, she was dissatisfied. It told much about Chinese life, but she felt that it was too sentimental and that much of the language was undisciplined. She packed it away in the bottom of her trunk and, in the many pressing things that needed to be done the next few months, nearly forgot about it.

Nine

❧

Anything Can Be Destroyed

At a famous medical clinic in the United States a doctor told Pearl that Carol would never be normal. The child's body would grow physically but her mind would remain forever that of a child of four. She was the victim of an inborn disorder that had affected her brain. Today doctors have developed treatment for this disease and, if they detect it in time, know how to prevent the brain injury—but such measures were unknown in 1925.

The doctor told her that for her own sake and Carol's she must not let her child consume her. She must live her own life, he said, and it would be best to find a home for retarded children where Carol would receive experienced care and be happier.

But Pearl could not yet take that step. She took the poor little child back to the house rented near Cornell University. It seemed too much to bear. She had a great need to have children about her, to see them grow, to love them and be loved by them, to share her life with them. There was nothing of love's deep language between her and John—Was she forever to be denied this, even from the only child she could ever bear? This was a low point in her life.

Somehow during this time she concentrated on her studies, devouring books by the dozen during the free hours of the day and far into the night. An understanding professor permitted her to skip many classes and work on her own, which was a blessing, because she had so many things to do for Carol and John. It was a pinched time, for John's meager income, while enabling them to live comfortably in China, barely kept them in food in America. She bought food directly from farmers in order to save money, and she was able to manage but one modest slice of meat a week. The bitter winter of northern New York was coming on and she did not even own a warm coat.

How to make money? She remembered the story she had written on shipboard and wondered if it were possible to sell it. Would readers be interested in a story about China? She dug it out, polished up the writing, typed it, and sent it off to *Asia Magazine*. Almost immediately she received from the editor a letter of acceptance and a payment of one hundred dollars.

The money never went for a coat, but was eaten up by school fees and bills. She began another story, a sequel to the first. It involved the story of Kwei-lan's brother, who marries an American girl. His family refuses to accept the marriage; his mother becomes so depressed about it that she dies; and at last he wrathfully denounces his family and ancient traditions, and remains with the woman he loves. In the birth of their child is expressed the hope that some day East and West will learn to live together.

But the story went slowly, and Pearl still had no warm coat against the winter. "Quite cold-bloodedly" she asked which was the largest prize offered by the university for writing, and learned that it was for a historical theme. Against the advice of her English professor, who warned that the prize had always been won by someone in the history department, she set herself to work during a recess between semesters. The result was an essay, nearly book-length, on the impact of the West on Chinese life and civilization. She submitted it, and two weeks later came the notice that she had won. The prize was two hundred dollars, which seemed to her a fortune, more than enough to see the family through the rest of the winter and to provide her with a warm, soft, green coat.

Now, more uplifted in heart, she determined that she would have a family after all.

She went from one adoption agency to the other, begging for a child to adopt as her own, but the agencies refused to give away a baby who would soon be taken to such a heathen corner of the earth as China. At last a friendly Presbyterian minister took her to a small orphanage whose director was willing to give her a baby. "Take your choice," he said, pointing to twenty cribs in the nursery. Pearl went down the line of cribs and stopped at last, her heart caught by pity, at one exquisite little creature, tiny as a toy, who lay with closed eyes, scarcely breathing.

"How old is she?" Pearl asked.

"Three months," said the director, "and she has never gained since birth. She will not eat."

"I want her," Pearl said.

The director argued against it. The child was doomed, he said. Why invite tragedy? But Pearl insisted. She bundled up the delicate little burden and took it home. There, like a bud brought to the sun, the infant Janice responded to Pearl's affection, began to eat and grow. In only two weeks she was actually plump. Pearl's family, which was eventually to grow to nine adopted children, was on its way. Motherhood would not be denied her.

Things were looking up. She finished the story about Kwei-lan's brother, sent it off to *Asia Magazine,* and it was accepted. The year of despair had ended in triumph. She had confidence now, more than enough to tide her over one publisher's refusal (possibly the most costly mistake he ever made) to publish her two stories together as a book. The Bucks packed their few belongings and, with two children now, returned to China.

Even on the voyage home she began writing her first novel. Back in China she found in a small shop an ancient Chinese desk, solid as a house, its wood a warm chocolate glow, its broad surface inviting. This was indeed a proper desk for a writer—a *published* writer, no less! She bought it and installed it in her attic room in Nanking.

China was troubled. The uprisings of the past had failed, corruption in government was again the fact, and warlords continued to tear the country apart. Now a new revolution was brewing. The Communists were joining with a group called the Kuomintang, led by General Chiang Kai-shek, to overthrow the warlords and bring a new rule. Already some northern cities had exploded into combat, and rumors filtered south of the killing of white foreigners, an inevitable event whenever the deep anger of the oppressed Chinese caught flame.

By the spring of 1927 the revolutionary armies were poised above Nanking, and the city lay waiting for their advance. Ahead of them came Pearl's sister Grace with her husband and baby, fleeing the troops. All whites of Nanking were urged by the American consul to escape while there was yet time. However, Pearl and others decided to stay with their Chinese friends. They were in sympathy with the aims of the uprising even though they knew the danger to foreigners, regardless of their sympathies, when soldiers ran amok. Absalom, of course, would not budge; he felt more Chinese than American anyway.

But one day in March the soldiers marched on the city, and it became apparent that the danger to foreigners was greater than had been believed. News came to the Buck household that the soldiers were killing white people and plundering their homes. Already the vice-president of the Christian university lay dead in the street. Pearl and her family left the fire burning in the stove, breakfast half eaten on the table, and ran across the fields seeking a place to hide. Mrs. Lu, a poor woman whose infant son Pearl had once saved from death, ran to gather them in her arms. She drew them into her own thatched mud hut and hid them there.

There they huddled through the day and the night. Through a crack under the roof they could see the red glow in the sky where the seminary burned. And they could hear the shouts of the soldiers and the mob as the door to their own house splintered and the rooms were invaded.

Pearl winced, remembering that on her desk in the attic room lay the finished manuscript of her first novel.

Outside their hiding place they heard running feet, the songs of marching soldiers, the crackle of flames, and the rumble of falling walls. Then, when night came again, they heard a new sound, that of a huge cannon. The Chinese had no such weapons; surely the guns must be from foreign warships that had come up the river. Would they be saved or would they die under the artillery shells?

They were discovered. Soldiers burst in on them and, prodding them with bayonets, led them out into the streets

toward the university where white prisoners were being collected. At one moment little Carol stumbled and pushed a
soldier, who turned snarling on her with his bayonet. Pearl
pleaded for her baby's life, and in her memory she recalled the
time many years earlier when Caroline had so pleaded for her.

At the university were other white prisoners, most of them
saved so far because they had been protected by Chinese friends.
They had seen killing; some were wounded or beaten. Now,
it turned out, the commander of the warships on the river was
negotiating with the Chinese generals for the release of the
whites. At last the prisoners were gathered and brought down
to the riverside where the warships lay waiting. It was strange,
thought Pearl, to be saved by these ships now; she had always
resented them, been ashamed of their presence.

The refugees were taken aboard an American destroyer,
which then raced down the river to Shanghai. They were
hardly welcome aboard the destroyer. The sailors were surly
and short of temper with this ragged band of refugees; they
hated being in a foreign land and resented being endangered
by this group of missionaries who had waited until the last
moment to escape from certain danger.

Stepping off the ship at Shanghai, Pearl felt a sudden
sense of freedom. Everything of the past was lost. She owned
nothing but the clothes she wore. Lost now were her books, her
fine desk, and the soft green coat so painfully earned. Even her
novel and her biography of Caroline were back in Nanking,
undoubtedly torn to shreds by the mob. She had no "home."
Strangely, she felt no grief. "Simply the fact was that nothing
was ever as valuable to me again, nothing, that is, in the way
of place or beloved objects, for I knew now that anything
material can be destroyed. On the other hand, people were

more than ever important and human relationships more valuable."

In such a mood she found Shanghai intolerable. She felt she needed a quiet place in which to live awhile, one that had no claim on her loyalties or emotions, where she could review her life and determine where and how, if ever again, she would sink roots. Absalom, also testing his freedom, insisted on going alone to Korea to see what could be done in missionary work there.

The Bucks went to Japan and there, sustained by John's small salary from the mission board, found a little house high in the hills above Nagasaki. There, in quiet, clean Japan, among mountains wreathed in mists and twisted pines she found tranquility. It was an opportunity, too, to get to know the Japanese people, whom she found kind and exquisitely courteous. Yet she noted that there was a wild and brutal strain that lay deep, coming to the surface when too much liquor cracked the disciplined behavior of the Japanese men.

By winter it seemed safe to go back to China. The Nationalist Party, under Chiang Kai-shek's leadership, had gained the upper hand. They had turned on their Communist allies, were eliminating them from positions of power, and had declared war on them. Also, Chiang Kai-shek was being friendly to the Western powers and seeking their support.

Returning to China, Pearl found that Nanking was still considered not completely safe, and it would be necessary to stay awhile in Shanghai. She hated it. The city was thronged with rich Chinese and white refugees, equally contemptuous of the massed and starving poor. As for the news from the rest of China, it was sickening to hear of Chiang Kai-shek's brutality toward the Communists and others who disagreed with him.

Again under the Nationalists there existed corruption in government, heavy taxes on the people, contempt for the common man, imitation of the West, privilege, and misuse of power—the same sad old Chinese story.

Pearl wrote to a friend: "This cannot go on forever. Personally, I feel that unless something happens to change it, we are in for a *real* revolution here, in comparison with which all this so far will be a mere game of ball on a summer's afternoon. Then it will be a real uprising of the ignorant and poor, against those who own anything."

In a bookstore in Shanghai she found a dog-eared little book called *The Writer's Guide,* which listed the names of literary agents, people who deal with publishers and attempt to sell the works of writers. She wrote to two of them. One, David Lloyd, asked to see her material, and she sent him the two Kwei-lan stories that had been printed in *Asia Magazine,* suggesting that together they might make a book.

At last it was safe to return to Nanking. Absalom had already returned quietly and was living there with Chinese friends. The Bucks went back to the house, which had fortunately not been destroyed, although it was emptied of valuables. The grand old desk was still in the attic, however, bearing a few scars. The novel that had lain on it was scattered to the winds. A few household objects had been saved from the mob by Chinese neighbors and some of Pearl's students, who had pretended to loot them but instead had stored them away. Among such effects was the mansucript of *The Exile,* Caroline's biography, still safe in its box.

So it was the same, and yet not the same. She put her house in order and returned to the university to teach. But there were missing seats in her classes, and when she inquired, she found that some of these students had been arrested and some put to death for being Communists or for reading liberal magazines or for criticizing Chiang Kai-shek. China was in the grip of a hard, military rule.

Another duty lay ahead. She made the decision at last to put Carol into a home and school for retarded children, and this meant a swift journey back to the United States in 1929.

Saddened after leaving Carol, she stayed a few weeks with friends in Buffalo. She received a cable there. It had been sent to China from New York and then had been forwarded back to her in the United States. It was from her agent, David Lloyd. Her Kwei-lan stories had been accepted as a book under the title *East Wind: West Wind*. Lloyd had sent it to every publisher in town, and this had been the last hope before giving up. Could she come to New York to discuss some changes?

Her agent and the publisher, the John Day Company, had expected that she would come flying in excitement the moment she received the news, as would any new writer at the acceptance of a first book. But Pearl had been raised in China, where time was forever, and there was always enough of it to wait a little longer. Flabbergasted, they waited weeks before Pearl found the time to come down to New York City from Buffalo.

The chief editor of the publishing firm was Richard J. Walsh, a lanky, handsome man with bright, interested blue eyes and a courtly manner. He explained that the book had great promise but would need some editing, for it contained stiff and "purple" language that seemed to be in imitation of other writers. Why didn't she write in a manner that was true to herself? Astounded, Pearl explained that in China it was considered good form to imitate the classics. But she understood exactly what he meant and agreed to the necessary changes.

To Walsh, Pearl surely seemed one of the most fascinating women he had ever met. At first he had thought that her delay in coming and her innocence about the world of publishing and business was staged. But now he knew it was real. Handsome and large-boned, with those incredible ice-blue eyes, Pearl Buck had none of the coquettish ways so many attractive women in his experience affected. She dressed plainly, wore no makeup, combed her hair simply, and talked in a direct fashion without pretense of any sort. She had a quiet and calm about her that seemed from another world, indeed, from Asia. There was iron in this woman's soul, and it stirred him. Yes, he would publish her book and wait eagerly for the next one.

Pearl returned directly to China. With only Janice to care for, there was so much less to do in the house. Even Pearl had not realized how much of her energy and time Carol had drained away. Now that energy and care, released from a great sad weight, burst forth seeking new targets.

She cleared away the great square desk in the attic, faced it to the mountain, and began to write the book that would be known as *The Good Earth.*

Ten

The Good Earth

The book poured out like a damburst. Its people and events, released now from long captivity in her mind, seemed to know exactly where to go and what to do. These were the people from the farms around Nanhsüchou, rooted like radishes in the earth. They were the peasants of China, unable to read or write and therefore without voice or power, remembered by the nation's rulers only as a source of taxes and toil. They were forgotten now while the nation's warring factions struggled for power.

The peasants were 85 percent of the people, its great silent bulk, despised for their ignorance. But Pearl knew that they were not ignorant and that the ability to read and write and imitate the language of scholars did not automatically bring wisdom or even sensitivity. The peasant might not read, but he spoke a rich language, lived in a complicated and ancient order of things, was wise in the ways of men, shrewd in the ways of survival, and had a deep sense of his own worth and dignity.

Especially now, Pearl felt, was it important to tell the story of the peasant, who could not and would not tell his own. She would have to find a style and attitude of writing as direct and natural as that of the Chinese peasant himself. Only a simple approach could, like clear glass, show how human and complicated he was.

In three months she had finished the book. Her brother Edwin was in China that year on a mission for a philanthropic organization for which he now worked, but Pearl was too shy to ask his opinion of her work. As for her father, Absalom, he had never read a book of fiction in his life and would surely not begin now. Her husband, John, was no reader at all, nor did she feel his opinion would be useful. She wrapped up the manuscript, bound it carefully, and sent it to her agent in New York.

David Lloyd, her agent, and Richard Walsh, her publisher, were then treated to a book the likes of which they had never read before. *The Good Earth* tells the story of Wang Lung, a farmer in need of a wife to care for him and his aging father. It is arranged for him to marry a bondmaid, O-lan, who is a slave of the local rich family. They are willing to let O-lan go for a small price because, although she is a good worker, she is ugly. But Wang Lung does not expect a pretty woman, poor and humble as he is, and he leads her home.

He is content, for O-lan has a hearty body, she is capable of untiring labor, and it turns out that she has far more common sense and shrewdness than her former owners credited her. With his strong wife at his side, working in the fields and bearing his children, Wang Lung begins to prosper, even to the point of laying enough money aside to purchase more land. The land is his life and strength; he loves it and feels himself part of it.

But hard times come, with severe drought and the failure of the crop. All around, peasants are dying of starvation. In order to survive, Wang Lung and O-lan leave the farm and wander south to the big city to try to find work. They live in a crude lean-to built against the city wall, while Wang Lung begs for pennies and works as a laborer and ricksha coolie. Around him he sees the luxury of the rich and feels their arrogance. O-lan begs, too, and between them they survive. When the fury of the poor erupts into rebellion and an outbreak of looting, Wang Lung is swept along. A frightened rich man, caught alone with Wang Lung, thinks he will be killed and pours all his money into Wang Lung's hands. During the riot, O-lan, wise to the ways of the rich, finds a small fortune in precious stones hidden behind loose bricks in a wall.

Their new riches enable them to leave the city and return home. Wang Lung can see only one thing to do with the money: to buy land. Thus, he purchases the acres of the rich family that had once owned O-lan, for they have now fallen on hard times because of their own weakness, idleness, and dissipation with opium. A big landowner now, Wang Lung hires workers, himself setting the pace for their labor, and becomes the wealthiest farmer in the district and a man of considerable influence.

In middle age, still strong and vigorous but unable to work on his own land because of his high station, he becomes restless. He seeks stimulation in pleasure houses and falls in love with Lotus, one of the women there. Unable to be without her, he brings Lotus home and sets her up in his household as his concubine, to O-lan's great humiliation and grief. In his home Lotus lives like the flower for which she is named, doing no work, idling all day, demanding jewels and money, and getting fat.

Raised in luxury, Wang Lung's sons have no contact with

the good earth that has been Wang Lung's source of strength. The oldest son, spoiled and without roots, becomes involved with his father's concubine, and Wang Lung, in a rage, sends him out of the house and arranges for his marriage to the daughter of a rich family. The second son is shrewd and businesslike; his heart is with the gaining and spending of money, not with the land.

O-lan, exhausted from a life of toil, dies, and Wang Lung is left alone. In his old age he tires even of Lotus, but he finds fresh love in a gentle little slave girl, only to outrage his third and youngest son, who desires her also. The boy, a tempestuous and strong-willed lad, leaves home to become a soldier. As Wang Lung nears his end, his two older sons rival each other for status and plan how they will sell the land and divide the proceeds between them when their father dies.

The book was a remarkable performance by a writer in full command of her material and her style. The details of Chinese life made up the rich texture of the story—the earthen houses and their fragrance, the smell of the fields and hills, the customs and manners in the homes of rich and poor, the cities bursting with humanity, corruption, toil, poverty, and wealth.

The book's style was ageless; it could have been translated from the Chinese ancients or from the Bible, and it was perfectly suited to the timeless sweep of the story. It was indeed like a book of the Bible with its strong roots in the land, its basic passions of love, jealousy, greed, family turmoil, and in the stately march of the story. Plague, locust storm, famine—all were there. The book's treatment of sex and affairs of the body was frank and open, like the Chinese, like the Bible, and unlike anything in American literature. Somehow it seemed to readers that this epic story, like that of the Bible, could be told in no other way.

Wang Lung is no usual hero. His is the soul of the Chinese peasant. He can work like a beast. He can be courageous, but he can also quake with fear. He can be tender, but he can also be coarse and unfeeling. He can be shrewd and cunning. But above all he is boisterously alive and intends to remain alive in spite of everything. His enormous vitality feeds on the land, his good earth, while those who leave the land lose their strength. In O-lan, her total gift of herself, her patience and endurance, Pearl fashioned a loving and unforgettable portrait of the Chinese peasant woman, scorned for her sex and treated as a beast of burden, but remaining the rock foundation of Chinese peasant life.

Richard Walsh and his publishing company lost no time rushing the manuscript into print. The book immediately won the reading public. It seemed just right for the times, even though it dealt with strange customs in a faraway land. Most Americans had only a dim notion of what the Chinese people were really like. In this sense the book furnished a view of of something fresh and romantically distant; Americans struggling through hard times found that the story took them for a while out of their own anxious lives, for the country was in the grip of a great depression then. But at the same time the story brought reality, too, and there were many American readers who felt a kinship with Wang Lung's struggles and with his great basic love for the land. *The Good Earth* seemed to have something to say to all—the rich and the poor, the readers and the seldom-readers, the young and the old, those seeking merely entertainment and those looking for better understanding of the world's variety. All sensed that the world was changing, even as the winds of change chilled Wang Lung's last days.

At bookstores and through book clubs, *The Good Earth* climbed to the top of the best-sellers list, stayed there, and would remain there longer than any book had ever done before. When informed by cable how well her book was doing, Pearl was overjoyed but yet did not know how much money was involved. Shyly she showed the printed volume to her father, who turned it in his hands as if it were an amusing but rather unimportant toy.

"How much money do you think you will make from this book?" he questioned, wondering also when she had found the time to write it.

"Oh, about twenty thousand dollars," Pearl answered. Even she had no idea she would earn more than a million dollars from it.

"That's a lot of money for a novel," said Absalom. "That's very nice, I'm sure, but I'm afraid I can't undertake it." He was unable to bring himself to read fiction, and thus he never read any of his daughter's works.

Well, that was Absalom, and she had come to love and respect that single-mindedness of his. Even if his lack of interest had hurt her, there was very little time to fret about it or even to speculate how rich the book might make her. She was too deeply immersed in other writing.

In a very short time she completed another book, *The Mother*. This told the tale of a peasant woman, a type known throughout the world, spending her life in toil, receiving no fulfillment except to know that she survived. A shiftless husband runs away and leaves her to labor in the fields and raise their children. In her loneliness she has a brief romance with a land agent, but he leaves her, too. A daughter becomes blind, and this grieves her. Her favorite, her youngest son, becomes a revolutionary, and when he is caught by the authorities, he is killed. The blind daughter, married off, is mistreated by her husband and dies. The mother is left an old woman, with nothing to do, living with her oldest son and his wife, at last taking hope in the birth of her first grandchild.

The book is written in as simple and undecorated language as Pearl could use. She was determined never again to earn the charge of "purple writing" that had been leveled against *East Wind: West Wind*. Yet, when she was finished with *The Mother* she felt unsatisfied with it. Something seemed wrong. In sudden despair she threw the manuscript into the wastebasket. Fortunately the house servant was ill that day and the next, so that the wastebasket was not emptied—leaving Pearl time to reconsider, recover the pages and reread them. Still in doubt, she did not throw the manuscript away the second time but instead put it away for a few years.

When it was published some three years later, in 1934, there were some who felt that it needed more careful rewriting to smooth out some of the sharp, unexplained changes in the flow of the story. Some readers had no sympathy with or understanding for the principal character. Nevertheless there were readers all over the world who saw their own lives in it or the lives of women they knew.

But in 1931 Pearl was already launched into two projects. One was a sequel to *The Good Earth*. Titled *Sons,* it continued the story of Wang Lung's family. At the same time she undertook to translate into English a great and ancient Chinese novel, *Shui Hu Chuan,* or *All Men Are Brothers*. All day the gleaming Mandarin desk in the attic vibrated to the sound of a scratching pen.

In the mornings she worked on *Sons*. In the afternoons she translated *Shui Hu Chuan*. Somehow during these hours and in the evenings she managed also to perform as housekeeper, mother, wife, and daughter. There was more money now, and she could afford housekeeping help, but she preferred to keep strong control because her home was always important to her. She found hours to attend to Janice's needs, helping with schoolwork and participating, as Caroline had done, in her daughter's learning. There was Absalom, worn frail and nearly as transparent as a spirit, to care for. The fear of death had come to him and she needed to see that he felt constantly cherished, that he was kept warm, tucked in at night, involved in the affairs of the house, and in touch at all times with the sounds and sights of life.

And there was John, forever "collecting his data" on Chinese farm life, needing to feel important, and also needing guidance in organizing his material. In the last few years he had become very dependent on her. He had begun to complain of not being able to bear light, and he constantly wore dark glasses. Pearl sewed window shades out of dark cloth to keep the light out of the house. He grew worse and said he could not even read. It became Pearl's job to read the books he needed for his work and explain the contents to him.

Sometimes the burdens seemed too many. Everyone relied on her strength, and she had enough of that to spare, but frequently she tired of that role and wished there were someone to whom she, too, could go for comfort and guidance. Up in the attic at her desk, the Purple Mountain darkly gleaming in the distance, she felt free and she yearned for a way of life built around this free part of herself, a life without the duties that crowded her. If only one could follow one's desires and turn aside unwanted responsibilities! Then she felt guilt for such thoughts.

In the spring of 1932, in his eightieth year, Absalom died. He had gone to stay the summer at Kuling with Grace and her family. He contracted dysentery and, his body wasted to a "pearly shell," he passed away quickly. It took at least a week for the message to get through to Pearl, for fierce floods blocked the way and tore down the telegraph poles. By that time Absalom was already buried on a mountaintop, alone with swirling mists and the wind.

It was time to go back to America. Pearl's publisher, Richard Walsh, was begging her to come to receive the recognition and bask in the fame that *The Good Earth* had won her. Also, she felt the need to see Carol at the home where she had placed the child. And it was time for John to have another furlough. He wanted to spend some more time at Cornell University in order to complete his Ph.D. degree. While there, now that there was money to do so, they could also consult an eye specialist about John's failing sight. She packed her completed novel *Sons* and the translation *All Men Are Brothers,* arranged to rent a house in Ithaca near the university, and left for the United States by boat to Canada. Richard Walsh met them in Montreal.

One of her first obligations in America was to appear at a huge banquet in her honor, celebrating the breaking of all publishing records by *The Good Earth*. Nearly two million copies had been sold. New York's critics, writers, and editors were intensely curious about her. Many could not believe that an untrained woman, living all her life in the world of missionaries, could have created such a monumental book. They scoffed at stories of her innocence in business matters and her ignorance of the publishing world. They felt sure she was but an invention of her publisher.

The banquet, at the Waldorf-Astoria Hotel, was gala. Although it was August, literary figures interrupted vacations to come back to the city to attend. A great throng of them appeared—New York's most sophisticated and brilliant social group. The men were quick and well groomed. The women, indolently alert in evening gowns, wore their hair sleek in the close-cropped styles of the 1930's and their lips blazed with paint. Into this setting came Pearl, as curious about the audience as it was of her, but quaking with fear and shyness, too—perhaps for the first time in her life depending on a sensitive and thoughtful man, Richard Walsh, for courage and support.

An editor who was there still remembers it vividly. "And there was Pearl Buck, the literary phenomenon, at last. Only one look and you knew that what her publisher said about her had to be right. She was a shy creature, and mousy, and looked about to run away. I remember a plain blue dress that she surely must have made herself, for nothing so unstylish could be bought in New York anywhere. It actually had sleeves— unheard-of at that time for evening wear—and a high V-neck. Her hair was parted in the middle and pulled up into a plain bun. But she had this exquisite skin and not a dab, not a snitch, of makeup. She looked exactly what she was in fact—a missionary's wife."

Pearl was too timid to make a speech. Instead she read her translation of the preface to *Shui Hu Chuan,* written five hundred years before. It spoke of the measure of time and said that there was a time for all things, for the writing of books and for talk among friends, and that the latter was the more important of these, even more important than fame.

> Alas, I was born to die! How can I know of what those who come after me and read my book will think of it? I cannot even know what I myself, born into another incarnation, will think of it. I do not even know if I myself afterwards can even read this book. Why, therefore, should I care?

Retreating to the rented home in Ithaca, Pearl saw her adopted daughter enrolled in an American school, set up the house to her liking, and helped John with his studies. She also saw to it that John went to see a famous eye doctor.

After a week of testing, the doctor, an elderly man with wide experience, took Pearl aside and told her, "There is nothing wrong with his eyes. The trouble springs from the desire to monopolize your attention and to avoid the trouble of reading. He has never really mastered reading. Ignore him when he complains, gradually take away the shades at the windows, and be too busy to read. He monopolizes you."

This she did. John gradually grew better, as the doctor had predicted. One burden eased, she began to wonder, inevitably, what it would be like to shed more of this load. She was forty years old and had been married for seventeen years to a man for whom she felt nothing but habit and a nagging obligation to look after his needs. Would it be possible to go on this way and still follow where her writing seemed to be taking her?

She went down to New York City frequently, for there were many people there who wanted to meet her. She formed close friendships with stimulating and cultivated people—

writers, editors, artists, musicians. She was surprised to find, however, that in the United States, unlike in China or Europe, there was no real community of writers who made it a point to stay in touch with one another.

She spent much of her time with Richard Walsh. They frequently had lunch together to discuss her writing plans and business obligations. It was a joy to talk to him. Walsh was sensitive to what went into the creation of a novel and he had a sharp editor's eye for ways of improving language, organizing material, and eliminating what was unimportant. He knew every corner of New York, and it seemed to her that he knew every New Yorker, too. He helped her with her speeches and arranged for her to meet people who would be important to her. He was knowledgeable about Asia as well as about many other subjects, and never at a loss for some perceptive thing to say.

What a pleasure to depend on someone else for a change! Pearl basked in the luxury of it. She wrote him in a note: "Sympathy and understanding appreciation are so delightful— I am not used to them—and it is for me wonderful—I mean, so far as my work is concerned, I have not since my mother died years ago lived among people who value such things or consider them of importance or who understand my supreme interest in writing."

But if she became too serious, Walsh had a way of making her laugh with a funny remark. His own smile began in his startling blue eyes and then spread across his always sunburned face.

One day, Richard Walsh told her he loved her and wanted to marry her.

"We are both married and have children," she exclaimed. "It's unthinkable!"

"Do you think I like it?" he replied. "Here I am, a publisher, and I've fallen in love with my best-selling author! Stupid of me!" He pointed out, however, that both of their marriages were unsatisfactory even after a long trial. A second chance at happiness was now theirs to seize—provided, of course, that she was in love with him, too.

She was.

Edwin, Pearl, and Grace Sydenstricker with their mother.
Elliott Erwitt/Magnum.

Chinese peasants at work in a rice paddy in Kwangsi province.
Marc Riboud / Magnum.

Shanghai harbor. *Henri Cartier-Bresson / Magnum.*

A contemporary engraving of the Boxer Rebellion.
Frederick Lewis, Inc.

Street scene—Shanghai. *Henri Cartier-Bresson/Magnum.*

Pearl Buck and her daughter, Carol, in Nanking. *Brown Brothers.*

Pearl and John Buck
returning to the
United States in 1932.
This snapshot was
taken aboard ship as
they crossed the
Pacific. *Wide World
Photos.*

Pearl Buck receives the Nobel award from King Gustav of Sweden, 1938. *Wide World Photos.*

Richard Walsh correcting a manuscript. *Courtesy, New York Public Library Picture Collection.*

A scene from the motion picture, *The Good Earth. Springer/
Bettmann Film Archive.*

The house in Bucks County, Pennsylvania. *Elliott Erwitt/Magnum.*

Pearl Buck with two of the children at
Welcome House. *Culver Pictures, Inc.*

Pearl Buck at seventy-five, in her study in Philadelphia with a bound copy of *Asia Magazine,* which she directed during World War II. *Wide World Photos.*

Ernest Hocking.
Wide World Photos.

Eleven

❧

A New Life

She could not make up her mind to leave her husband. One day she was determined to do it; the next it seemed impossible.

In most things Pearl had always managed to do exactly as she wanted. She thought according to her own lights, and she wrote as she saw the world. But in matter of arrangements among people—the obligation to family, the direction of a home, the contract of marriage—she found it hard to break with ancient rhythms. She had always felt deeply that she was part of an immense current of life, a link between the long past and the far future.

Also, in the back of her mind still raged a struggle between her allegiance to China and her allegiance to America, and it was hard to choose between them. By training and outlook she felt more Chinese than American, and she loved the land and the people among whom she had spent almost all her life, but yet she was not even sure that she was safe in revolution-torn China.

Although she had seen much in America that charmed and stimulated her, she had also seen things that horrified her and made her wonder if she could indeed feel at home there. Even her reading about the role of black people in American life had not prepared her for the way she would feel when she saw the effects of race prejudice firsthand.

Late in the year she was invited to an exhibition of paintings by black Americans. As she moved from one picture to the other, confusion and then shock overcame her. She wrote, describing the event: "The paintings were of unimagined horrors. I saw sad dark faces, I saw dead bodies swinging from trees, I saw charred remains of houses and tragic children. I saw narrow slum streets and slouching poverty-stricken people."

Were such things reality or nightmare? She demanded an explanation of the pictures on the spot. A crowd of people, white and black, gathered about her, and there and then Pearl Buck received a brief education concerning the life of the black man in white America. She heard about prejudice, lynching, segregation. The truth stunned her. She found herself weeping and speaking out angrily. Unless Americans practiced the principles of equality they preached, she demanded to know, how could they ever expect to be believed in the rest of the world, and how could they escape the certain punishment that Asia would soon wreak on the white man?

Greatly disturbed, she left the gallery and went home to stay alone for several days, "not wanting to see anyone or to hear a human voice until I had faced and understood the full meaning and portent of this monstrous situation in my own country, a situation which involved us in the whole danger of the white man in Asia, though it was on the other side of the globe." She read everything she could on the subject and sought the friendship of black men and women, the better to understand.

America or China? China's call was strong. She once said, "I write because it is my nature to do so, and I can write only what I know, and I know nothing but China, having always lived there. I have had few friends of my own race, almost none intimate, and so I write about the people I do know. They are the people in China I love best to live among, the everyday people."

The upshot of all these conflicts was that, when the sabbatical year was over, Pearl, John, and Janice returned to China. They went the long way east, taking time out to see some of England and Europe. The excitement and charm of the Old World did not erase Richard Walsh from her mind, however, or help her determine what to do. In Italy they boarded a ship for China, and it was during this voyage that she decided to tell John about her dilemma.

"Let me have one year in which to find out what I want to do with my life. Just one year with no promises, no ties, a year of complete freedom," she asked him.

John was thoroughly surprised. It had never occurred to him that their marriage was anything but a successful arrangement. In bewilderment he agreed to a separation. When they reached China, Pearl went on to the Nanking house. She had a novel in mind, but she could not make much progress writing it, so confused and divided were her feelings. One day Richard Walsh showed up. He had followed her to China. He begged her to return to America with him. She had missed him dreadfully, but still she insisted unhappily that she needed time alone with herself in order to sort out her feelings. Walsh left.

Pearl traveled through Asia. She went to the cities of China where she had not been before. She traveled to India, Indochina, Cambodia, Laos, Thailand, and everywhere she noted the greed and cruelty of European colonial powers and the rising wrath of the Asian against the white man. In India she met and talked with passionate young intellectuals who described to her their plan to strike against England for freedom the moment England became engaged in a new war. She visited Indian villages and spoke with the peasants. The depth of the poverty and starvation appalled her, and she was horrified to learn that the average life span in India was twenty-seven years. It amazed her that after three hundred years of English rule such primitive, impoverished conditions could exist. "And I was forced to see that if the English, in many ways the finest people on earth, a people who blazed the way for all of us to achieve the right of men to rule themselves, if colonialism could so corrupt even these, then indeed none of us could dare to become the rulers of empire."

Especially she came to admire the great gentleness of Indians, their reverence for wisdom, and the selflessness of their leaders.

Traveling back through China, near Peking, in order to do research for her translation *All Men Are Brothers,* she ran into Richard Walsh again. Again he asked her to marry him and again she said no. He went on into Manchuria, and she to her research.

When she returned to the house in Nanking, restlessness seized her. Walsh was much on her mind. She felt guilty for having been away so long from Carol who, according to reports from the home for retarded children, was having difficulty. Also, her restlessness was part of a world uneasiness, for she sensed war in the air, a great world upheaval that would engulf Asia, too, and forever change the role of the white man in that continent. Perhaps it was truly time to close the book of this first half of her life and begin again in a new home.

In the spring of 1934, then, with her adopted daughter and her secretary, she set sail for America. On the deck, as she worked at her translation, a clear and familiar voice broke through her concentration. "I've turned up again—I shall keep on turning up, you know—everywhere in the world. You can't escape me." It was Richard Walsh, lean and brown, eyes twinkling, puffing his pipe. He had boarded the ship at Yokohama. Every day across the Pacific and each day from Vancouver to New York he proposed, and each day she said no.

She later explained, "I still think I was so slow to make up my mind about marriage because the marriage I had, had never meant enough to me to convince me that any marriage would mean much to me. Now that doesn't mean that I didn't have deep and long friendships with men, because I did, but I found more outside of marriage than within it. . . . I had lived in a solitary sort of fashion all my life and I wasn't sure I needed marriage."

Whatever happened, she would need a home. Home to her meant her own house, a solid one. She wanted roots in America, and the cities did not give her all she needed. When driving to visit Carol, she frequently passed through Bucks County in Pennsylvania and it seemed like fine country, with rolling hills, rich woods, and trickling streams. The farmhouses seemed built to last forever, like Chinese houses, and she liked that. Before long she found an old stone farmhouse built in 1835, which she bought. It had fireplaces big enough to stand in, thick stone walls, heavy beams, wide oak floors, many-paned windows. It seemed a proper house; she did not trust one built of wood. She set craftsmen to work at restoring and improving the place, for it needed repair and such things as plumbing and electricity.

Sometime while she was arranging to buy the house, she decided at last to seek a divorce and remarry. The plans for the house began to include additional rooms for a nursery and bedrooms for the children she and Walsh planned to adopt. Now she would have the large family she had always wanted.

Pearl Buck and Richard Walsh obtained their divorces in Reno, Nevada, in the spring of 1935 and got married the next day. After a short honeymoon at Lake Tahoe they returned to the Pennsylvania farmhouse. If she had any doubts about having done the right thing, they were soon dispelled. She grew to love the house, felt rooted in its solid beams and old stones, and she was charmed and heartened by the kindness of her neighbors and their respect for her privacy. Most important of all was the unaccustomed joy of living with a man whose mind was close to her own in scope, curiosity, and vitality. No more the long silences, with nothing to talk about. In this new house and life, books and knowledge were revered, her work was respected. Walsh was a man of flashing wit and high humor—and he brought new fun and gaiety into Pearl's life.

There would, of course, always be that secret, private castle keep inside herself, but she no longer felt it was under attack.

Not that she and Richard Walsh agreed on everything, for they did not. Although Pearl claimed no formal religion, she felt strongly drawn to spiritual matters. Her Asian background and religious training led her to feel that there was much in life that could not be explained by reason and fact alone, and that there was an important role for spirit, for soul, and for mystery. She constantly wondered what was beyond what the eye could see, the hand could feel, and the reasonable mind could affirm. But Richard Walsh was a realist who searched for the scientific explanation, scoffed at visions as hysteria, scorned religion of any type, and distrusted what many felt to be affairs of the spirit. He was deeply interested in political matters, even though he sourly doubted man's ability to improve himself. For such a pessimist about human nature he was nonetheless a soft touch for anyone who needed help, and he was frequently taken advantage of by acquaintances, to Pearl's anger.

He always knew how to tease her. She was unlike any woman he had ever known, he would say, because she had the brain of a man in the body of a woman. Always she rose to the bait and flew at him—Did Nature give fine minds only to men, was intelligence a male trait only? Abjectly he would apologize, but with his eyes laughing.

Before long they visited the adoption agencies, and their new family began to grow. The large third-floor bedroom was turned into a nursery, occupied at first by two baby boys, Richard and Edgar, and, a year and a half later, by an additional baby boy and girl, John and Jean. Pearl and Richard threw themselves into the tasks of bottlewarming, diaper changing, and midnight bottles with all the enthusiasm of just-marrieds in their twenties. The babies went where they went, commuting with them between Bucks County and New York City, and the baby-laden car became familiar to toll operators, policemen, doormen.

It was a rich, busy, new life.

Twelve

☙

The Material of a Writer

During the period between the publication of *The Good Earth* and Pearl's marriage to Richard Walsh there were several important events in her literary career. The first of these was the winning of the Pulitzer Prize in 1932, the treasured award given annually for distinguished American writing. She received news of the award in China, and at that time she was still so unknowing about the American literary world that she did not fully understand its importance. But it did not take long for her to realize that it was extremely important to others, for immediately all sorts of critics and writers stepped forward to scold the Pulitzer Prize committee for having given the honor, which was supposed to be for the best American novel, to a writer who lived in China and wrote about the Chinese.

Such criticism bewildered her, and she did not spend much time answering it, nor did she know how. But on at least two subjects she felt she had to talk back, and she did.

One of these concerned the criticism that came from Chinese intellectuals living and studying in America. Why, they wondered, had she chosen to write about peasants like Wang Lung and not about educated and courtly people? And why

did she have to write about sex, bandits, famine, and the bind-
ing of women's feet? These were the worst aspects of Chinese
life, they claimed, and did not truly reflect life in China. She
was giving China a bad name.

Firmly, but not neglecting her Asian courtesy, Pearl
begged to differ. All the things she wrote about she had seen
with her own eyes, she insisted, and she provided details to
prove it. The great mass of China was its peasantry, she pointed
out, not the tiny fraction of well-to-do merchants and intellectuals. She knew the real China far better than did these intellectuals, who for thousands of years had shut themselves
off from the great seething bulk of China to live in the polite,
mannered little world of their own making. China's great
agony, and its future, could be found in this cleavage between
the ruled and the rulers.

"For shall the people be counted as nothing," she demanded in a *New York Times* letter in January 1933, "the
splendid common people of China, living their tremendous
lusty life against the odds of a calamitous nature, a war-torn
government, a small, indifferent aristocracy of intellectuals?
For truth's sake I can never agree to it."

She went on, "The point that some of China's intellectuals
cannot seem to grasp is that they ought to be proud of their
common people, that the common people are China's strength
and glory."

Another subject on which she felt she had to have her say
was the missionary movement. Many people were questioning
the need for the religious missions sent to China and other
lands. Among them was a group of prominent churchmen
headed by Dr. Ernest Hocking, professor of philosophy at Harvard University. Pearl had met Hocking many years before,

when he was in China doing research for a report on the missionary movement. She found him attractive and witty and with a quality of mind that excited her. He recognized in her at once a superior person who would someday make her mark. Now his report was out, severely criticizing the narrow-mindedness and bigotry of many missionaries. People now sought the views of the famous daughter of a missionary, Pearl Buck. She was glad to give her opinion; indeed, she had spent a lifetime preparing it. Her article describing missionary life, which was published in the January 1933 issue of *Harper's Magazine,* began with these words:

> I have seen the missionary narrow, uncharitable, unappreciative, ignorant. I have seen him so filled with arrogance in his own beliefs, so sure that all truth was with him and him only, that my heart has knelt with a humble one before the shrine of Buddha rather than before the God of that missionary, if that God could be true. I have seen missionaries, orthodox missionaries in good standing in the church—abominable phrase!—so lacking in sympathy for the people they were supposed to be saving, so scornful of any civilization except their own, so harsh in their judgments upon one another, so coarse and insensitive among a sensitive and cultivated people that my heart has fairly bled with shame. I can never have done with my apologies to the Chinese people that in the name of a gentle Christ we have sent such people to them.

If there were any real need for foreign missions, she pointed out, it lay not in religious preaching but in loving attention to the sick and the poor.

The article caused an uproar, and Pearl was accused of heresy by some churchmen. She obliged by resigning as a missionary of the Presbyterian church, and she explained that she believed not in creeds and formal religion but in brotherhood, justice, and mercy. A religion or society that could not practice what it preached was not fit to lead.

During this time her book *Sons* appeared. A sequel to *The Good Earth,* it is concerned with the fortunes of Wang Lung's sons. The first son, Wang the Eldest, wants only riches and pleasure while the second son, Wang the Second, is a cunning businessman caring only for his profits. Both have lost the essential honesty of heart and the great energy that together with Wang Lung's firm roots in the land brought their peasant father from rags to riches. At his deathbed these two sons can only think of the riches they will inherit—and Wang Lung, knowing their thoughts, dies in weariness and disgust.

The youngest Wang, now a military officer, arrives after the old man's death. He wants no property, only money. Of all the sons, it is he who seems to have inherited most of his father's energy and single-mindedness. But where Wang Lung's drive was to accumulate land, the youngest son scorns such roots and wants only power over men. His ambition is to become a military leader. Strong and crafty, aided by the money he has inherited, he manages to assemble his own little army of soldiers. As a bandit leader, eventually known as Wang the Tiger, he wars on other bandits and so builds his power to the point where he becomes the official warlord for the region, constantly fighting for his territory against rivals.

He loves and takes for his wife the mistress of a rival bandit leader he has killed. When she betrays him by attempting to set up a competing army he kills her, too, and from then on he hates all women. All his love and affection becomes concentrated on his son Yuan, and his life is consumed by a campaign to mold this boy into a great warrior, even fiercer and stronger than himself. He gives the lad fine weapons and horses and surrounds him with instructors in the art of soldiering. But, just as long ago Wang the Tiger rejected his father, Yuan now rejects him. The boy hates weapons and the military life. He sees his father not as a fine warrior but merely as a bandit and a symbol of what is wrong with China. He is curious about the land and the farming life and, after leaving military school, even wants to return to the little earthen house where his grandfather began. Wang the Tiger, in fury and frustration, understands that he has failed. It is as if his own rejected father, Wang Lung the farmer, has come from his grave to revenge himself by claiming the Tiger's dearest possession. And so the story ends.

Pearl had drawn from her wide experience to portray yet another segment of Chinese life—the world of bandits and warlords, those fierce figures who held such a tight stranglehold on China's destiny and who needed to be swept aside before China could become a modern nation. There were many real-life models for Wang the Tiger, and his attitudes about life, women, and war were Chinese to the core. Also, his conflict with his son was another side of the battle between the old and the new, the war of the generations, that was splitting China.

In many respects Pearl felt that *Sons* was her best book so far, but critics did not agree. Although sections of the book contained some of the most beautiful writing she had yet done, much of the rest of the book seemed to move too slowly, and many readers found that they did not care as much about the fortunes of Wang the Tiger as they had about those of his father in *The Good Earth*. Her writing, cast in the biblical-Chinese saga style, sometimes seemed forced and artificial in this new book, whereas it had seemed so right in the earlier one.

Both books are part of a trilogy, a series of three books. *The Good Earth* comes first; *Sons,* second; and *A House Divided,* third. The last book was published in 1935, the year she remarried. It centers about the fortunes of Yuan. After the quarrel with his warlord father Yuan seeks refuge in his grandfather's old earthen house. But he finds that he is not safe there, for his uncles and their families have fled to Shanghai in fear of the rebellious peasants, returning only with hired soldiers to collect their rents. Nor can Yuan fit into rural life. Since he does not depend on it, he sees farming as tranquil and romantic, but the peasants know it to be a hard and bitter struggle for survival.

Rootless, trying to find himself, Yuan makes his way to Shanghai and lives with his wealthy and fashionable relatives there. In one of the best sections of the book, Pearl Buck shows us through Yuan's experiences the great contrast between the lazy and luxurious lives of the rich and the miserable toil of the poor. Unbelievable luxury and mindless extravagance exist as islands in a sea of disease, starvation, poverty, and death in the streets. The rich live with contempt, and the poor with hatred.

Influenced by a cousin, Meng, Yuan joins a band of revolutionaries. He is betrayed, captured, and jailed. His wealthy family pays a bribe and obtains his release and passage to the United States. He stays in America for six years, studying for a doctoral degree, and soon forgets the poverty he has seen and the hard lives of the peasants.

A new revolution takes place in China, and Yuan goes back home. The poverty and ignorance in the countryside now embarrass him, and he is appalled by how much still needs to be done before China can grow. He finds his father, the Tiger, weak, his private army broken, and dying after being tortured by a rival bandit chief. He sees that the new government is inefficient, riddled with corruption, out of touch with the common people, and too much under the influence of foreigners. The old way has died and the new has truly not yet been born. The book ends with Yuan trying to accept his people as they are, for the nation like himself is in change, uprooted, unable to shake off the weight of the past, unable fully to seize the future.

A House Divided presented a vivid picture of China in turmoil and helped many of its worldwide readers to understand the forces at work in that nation and on the Chinese mind. But many critics felt it was the least successful of the three books of which it was part. The biblical style, so important to Wang Lung's story—himself a near biblical figure—did not fit the more complicated concerns of his grandson Yuan. In particular, it was not up to the task of describing modern America or Americans. The reader is less interested in Yuan, who seems pushed from one episode to the other, from attitude to attitude, merely because the author has a point to make and not because of anything growing naturally out of his character.

Pearl's translation, *All Men Are Brothers,* was issued in 1933, providing Western readers with their first exposure to the grand, ancient tradition of the Chinese novel, as rich as anything Western literature has produced. It also revealed much about the source of Pearl's own inspiration, for the brooding, realistic novels of old China were an important part of her literary heritage. Her translation is careful and loving, and the mark of excellence in translation is reached and surpassed in that the translator's work becomes invisible and it is the original author, steeped in his own times, who is there on the printed page.

The next year, 1934, she dug out the manuscript of *The Mother,* the book she had written right after *The Good Earth* and which she had nearly thrown away. She polished it up, gave it to her publishers, and it came out that same year with great success. Her style, so suited for elemental peasant life, was on sure ground.

But this was a period of great change for her. Torn between China and America, she was now choosing America as her home, obtaining a divorce, remarrying, settling in a new house, gathering a new and large family to raise. Above all, she needed to soak in how America felt, sounded, smelled.

The comments of critics set her thinking. She could reflect, as many writers have, that a writer's true nationality is his material, that it is where the writer lives. A writer's material is the stuff of his life—the sounds and sights he knows best, the language that styles his thinking and feeling, the people he has shaped and who shaped him. Pearl's material was in *The Good Earth, The Mother, Sons, A House Divided*—China and its folk, rooted in the past, boiling with change. Her material was earthen houses, quiet courtyards, formal manners, fierce bandits, haughty lords, humble peasants, the sound of gongs, the odor of dung and incense, the shrilling of peddlers in the streets, the wailing of the starved, the battle-cries of soldiers and revolutionists. For how long could such substance provide fresh stories for her books? Already people were unfavorably comparing everything she wrote to *The Good Earth.* There were times she wished she had never written it.

Were some of the critics right that she was not truly an "American writer," but basically a Chinese writer with the accident of American birth and language? Could she write about Americans?

But, actually, she had already written about an American —Caroline, her mother. She unpacked the yellowing manuscript and read it again. It could do with some polishing, but it was good; Caroline came alive in it, real, abundantly American. It occurred to Pearl then that the book needed a companion, a biography of her father, and she was ready to write it now. She did just that.

Now from the distance of time and the perspective of maturity, she could see Absalom clearly. She could write as lovingly of his flaws as of his virtues. The man himself, harsh in truth, appeared on her manuscript pages. In Absalom Sydenstricker (in the book she called him Andrew), she realized, was that special human force that sent men across oceans and continents and the reaches of space. In him the absolute sense of right was welded to a cause she now believed to be pathetically mistaken, but that was not important. The man was important, and this was one man who above all things was true to himself, heedful of no other will but his own and what he thought was God's, absolutely honest, incapable of deceiving anyone, innocent as a babe, crafty as a fox, harsh as a force of nature. These were the qualities the world had need of; there were too many followers, doubters, yielders, stoopers, manipulators.

One would expect difficulty from such a man as from the mountain, the wind, the rain. Pearl saw him, too, as the last of a breed of men who, thrilling to what they felt was God's call, went out to unite the world in their vision. Some were totally bigoted, some entirely ignorant, but some like Absalom were without contempt, except for ignorance, and valued human variety and the worth of each soul. They fought windmills, they sought impossible dreams, often they did harm, and it was pure folly all of it, but it was magnificent human folly and in these men and their women was the stuff of great stories.

To understand Absalom, as to understand Caroline, was to understand two extraordinary Americans. And now they could be introduced to the public, side by side yet separate as they had been in life. The biography of Caroline was called *The Exile* and that of Absalom was titled *Fighting Angel*. The two books were published in 1936 and were immediate triumphs. Many said that the biographies were even better than *The Good Earth*. "In deepest truth American," said *The New York Times*, ". . . an epic of our country." The critic Dorothy Canfield Fisher wrote, *"Fighting Angel* is a human document of tremendous meaning . . . a powerful, moving, searching, invitation to meditate deeply on human life."

Thirteen

❧

"I, Too, Tell of Gods!"

Caroline and Absalom Sydenstricker were American to the core, but they were Americans in China, and they were of an American past. Also, the books about her parents were biographies, and Pearl did not want to write more of these. She was a writer of fiction. "Fiction is a painting, biography is a photograph," she wrote in the *Chicago Tribune*. "I like the freedom of creative writing. I like choosing and making my own characters."

Could she write a novel about American characters, set in the American scene, in the here and now? The critics were waiting to see if she could, and indeed, so was she.

The first attempt to Americanize her writing was a mistake. Perhaps she tried too soon. Perhaps she took the wrong model. This was a novel that appeared in serial installments in *The Women's Home Companion. Now and Forever* was the sort of light and superficial fiction that one might expect of a hack writer turning out yards of sentimental sentences for quick publication. It was no worse, but certainly no better, than the dozens of serials that appeared each month on the magazine racks. In the writing trade, this market was known

as "the slicks" and the product was a "potboiler," and Pearl
had shown that she could make her way in this medium.

No doubt she needed money. It irked her to depend on
anyone, even her husband. What was wrong with writing for
money? And did not millions of Americans gobble up magazine stories like these, scorning more ambitious books, and
should she not write for the masses of the people? Perhaps so;
but her critics replied that her magazine serial was nonetheless
not worthy of Pearl Buck, author of *The Good Earth, The
Mother, The Exile, Fighting Angel,* and winner of the Pulitzer
Prize and of the William Dean Howells Medal of the American Academy of Arts and Letters. Of such a writer one expected writing that would set the pace for American letters,
not follow at some distance behind.

Questions like these outlined the burden of responsibility
Pearl would continue to carry as a writer for the rest of her
life. In the first few years following her second marriage the
burden seemed more than she was willing to undertake. The
temptation was sometimes strong to give up writing altogether
and with it the awful responsibilities of being famous. Instead,
she wished to devote herself entirely to this fresh opportunity
to be wife, mother, household manager. These were important
creative tasks, and she was good at them, and the chance to
perform them in an atmosphere of love had been denied her
until now.

But it wasn't enough, being what tradition said a woman
must be. She had made her own way for too long to change.
The need to write made her fingers twitch. And there was,
quite simply, a need for money. She needed household help,
her large correspondence required a secretary, and she had

become accustomed to living well. Richard Walsh was not wealthy, and he also had certain financial obligations elsewhere. For one, his publishing firm was near bankruptcy, having been badly mismanaged during his long pursuit of Pearl, and it sorely needed moneymaking best sellers, which Pearl Buck could provide.

By 1938 she had decided that she was first and foremost a writer. There was no reason for that to cause unhappiness to anyone dear—she could be woman, wife, and mother, too—but if it did, well, it was too bad but it did not change the basic fact. It was her way, not anyone else's, not necessarily for all women.

In that year she produced a book that summed up much of her feeling. Entitled *This Proud Heart,* it tells the story of Susan Gaylord, a woman of superior talent and energy, attempting to realize herself as artist, mother, wife, and daughter. Each of these roles is important to Susan, and she accomplishes each well. As the story begins, Susan finds that her talent at sculpture, as well as her exceptional mental qualities, is taking her far away from her loving but ordinary husband and friends. They depend on her, leaning on her strength, even while fearing what sets her apart from them, and they constitute a barrier that she must eventually hurdle if she is to express her gifts. She loves and pities her husband, and feels that homemaking and child-rearing are creative endeavors, too, and important to her life. She does not want self-fulfillment to conflict with love and home, but inevitably it does. Here Pearl Buck explores not only the problems of women in society but also those of the strong and gifted people of either sex—for the superior person must always, sadly, leave someone dear behind. When a woman has genius, the problem of freedom is even more difficult. What would be considered admirable ambition in a man is considered selfishness in a woman. When urged by a sculptor friend to give up everything for the sake of art and work, Susan decides against such a one-sided existence.

But fate—and the author!—abruptly reverses Susan's decision, for her husband dies. She moves with her children to France to study sculpture and begins to achieve recognition. She falls in love with and marries Blake Kinnaird, a wealthy American artist. Indulging in love, she devotes herself entirely to Blake's happiness and comfort.

But again she finds that the cost of this is the neglect of her own work. What is more, that cost seems deliberately imposed by Blake, who is jealous of her talent. Again she is being held back by a man who feels that her gifts threaten his masculinity. She finds out that Blake is involved with another woman, and that discovery frees her even while it anguishes her—she decides to strike out for herself. She rents a studio away from home and works there daily, alone, discovering new reaches of her talent and the great joy of creativity and work on her own terms. At the end of the story she breaks completely with Blake.

The year 1938 was a pivotal year for Pearl in yet another way. One day the news came that she had been awarded the Nobel Prize for literature. This award, presented by the king of Sweden to selected worldwide scientists, artists, and writers each year, is the highest honor that can be achieved. It is given in acknowledgment of a body of work and its importance to the world community. Pearl Buck had become by then one of the most widely translated writers in the world and surely one of the most popular. Her message of the world's essential oneness, of the need for peace and understanding among nations, of the dignity and worth of humble people, was clear.

In her own heart Pearl felt unworthy of the Nobel Prize. She wished it had been given to someone like Theodore Dreiser. Many others agreed and said that her body of work was not yet large enough for a judgment, that mere popularity was not the measure of excellence, and that the opinions of other American writers should have been weighed.

The Nobel Prize committee, of course, felt differently. The award was not being made on the basis of one book, *The Good Earth,* contrary to what most people thought. They had weighed the impact of the trilogy, *The Mother,* and—most importantly—the two biographies. Years later, the chairman of the committee wrote:

> The decisive factor in the Academy's judgment was, above all, the admirable biographies of her parents, the missionary pair in China—two volumes which seemed to deserve classic rank and to possess the required prospects for permanent interest. In addition, her novels of Chinese peasant life have properly made a place for themselves by virtue of the authenticity, wealth of detail and rare insight with which they describe a region that is little known and rarely accessible to Western readers. But as literary works of art the two biographies remain incomparable with anything else in Pearl Buck's both earlier or later production.

But at that moment criticism was strong and Pearl was sick at heart. In dread she went to a banquet in her honor given by the P.E.N., a writers' association, where she knew she would have to speak to the very people who were so opposed to the award. Humbly she told the audience that she was a mere teller of tales to amuse and make the hours pass more lightly, raised in China to believe that such a storyteller was not truly an important figure.

When she sat down, a gangling man with red hair and pocked face, sitting next to her, turned to her angrily. He was Sinclair Lewis, a novelist who eight years before had himself won the Nobel Prize in the face of much criticism. "You must not minimize yourself!" he scolded. "Neither must you minimize your profession. A novelist has a noble function." He warned that she should not heed what others said but go on writing as she felt right. "You must write many novels and let people have their little say! They have nothing else to say, damn them!"

Lewis's scolding had an enormous effect on her, for she greatly admired his writing. Never would she apologize for her work again.

More confident now, she left for Sweden to receive the prize, accompanied by Richard and his daughter Betty. She stopped in England and Denmark, but refused an invitation to visit Germany, for she would not accept the hospitality of that nation, then under Hitler, where democracy and freedom were being destroyed.

In Sweden, accepting the award, she made a speech that, in tracing the origin and growth of the Chinese novel, explained herself. "It is the Chinese and not the American novel which has shaped my own efforts in writing. My earliest knowledge of story, of how to tell and write stories, came to me in China," she began. She traced the development of the novel in China as a people's art, told in the language of the common people and not of scholars "because the common people could not read and write and the novel had to be written so that when it was read aloud it could be understood by persons who could communicate only through spoken words." The story was all—story and character. In keeping with this tradition she believed that the novelist's true place was in the street, with the people, noisy, ugly, imperfect, but real.

"I have been taught to want to write for these people," she concluded. "If they are reading their magazines by the million, then I want my stories there rather than in magazines read only by a few. For story belongs to the people. They are sounder judges of it than anyone else, for their senses are unspoiled and their emotions are free. No, a novelist must not think of pure literature as his goal. He must not even know this field too well, because people, who are his material, are not there. He is a storyteller in a village tent and by his stories he entices people into his tent. He need not raise his voice when a scholar passes. But he must beat all his drums when a band of poor pilgrims pass on their way up the mountain in search of gods. To them he must cry, 'I, too, tell of gods!' And to farmers he must talk of their land, and to old men he must speak of peace, and to old women he must tell of their children and to young men and women he must speak of each other. He must be satisfied if the common people hear him gladly."

Although every day, in a sense, is both an end and a beginning, that December day in Sweden in 1938 was a special end and a special beginning for Pearl Buck. "You must not minimize yourself," Sinclair Lewis had told her, and this day ended the making light of herself and it finished the doubts. The doubts were not important anymore. Now she was Pearl Buck, Nobel Prize winner, and there was no reason under the sun why she need do anything except in her own way. She need satisfy only her readers and herself. She would go on, surrounded by love and approval if possible, but if not possible, very well then—alone, like that character of her own creation, Susan Gaylord.

Fourteen

✦

Grand Parade of Books

From 1938 and the winning of the Nobel Prize to her eightieth birthday Pearl Buck wrote nearly seventy books.

Her books cover a wide range. They are about the Asian countries, the United States, romance, adventure, history, and her opinions about the world and its problems with war, bigotry, and imperialism. That tireless pen of hers, driven by an astounding energy, by one of the nation's most unusual minds, and by the unshakable decisions she had made about herself that year of the Nobel Prize, scratched away day after day. Beyond the mighty output of books there is probably a nearly equal library of newspaper and magazine articles, speeches, and pamphlets.

This is not the place to describe fully such a body of work. Skimming through those years, one can see the major themes that kept coming up over and over again in her books. They tell us something about the concerns that drove her.

There was, of course, the problem of "Americanizing" her writing both for style and for content. At one time she felt that no American novel of hers could possibly get a fair review because it had become almost a habit for critics to declare that she could not write well about American subjects and to compare every new book of hers with *The Good Earth*. So she decided to outwit the critics by using a pen name. Between 1945 and 1953 five books appeared by a brand-new author—"John Sedges."

Of these books, the first, *The Townsman,* is the most important. She traveled to Kansas to do research for it and dug deeply into the history of the frontier towns. Her husband helped, too, for he had grown up in Kansas. Of her novel, a Kansas newspaper critic said, "This book must have been written by one who has spent a lifetime in Kansas." The book became very popular with American readers.

As an historical novel about the settling of the West, *The Townsman* had an interesting and fresh point of view. Instead of centering attention on cowboys, blazing six-shooters, and marauding Indians, the book features the lives and struggles of those who truly did the settling and building—the quiet stay-at-homes who fought for order, civilization, and grace. The central character is Jonathan Goodliffe, a member of an immigrant English family. While the others range on to seek quick fortunes in land speculation and gold prospecting, Jonathan decides to stay put in the little mudhole settlement of Median, where he establishes a school and in time founds a stable and prosperous farming community. Throughout the book he is a force for decency and against ignorance, greed, race prejudice, and violence. Somewhat prissy and lacking in the more colorful manly qualities, he loses the girl he loves to his more romantic and aggressive best friend. He marries a hard-working but unlovely woman, and although there is no passion in this marriage he is loyal to it. His personal needs are second to the needs of the law-abiding town he has created.

The details of life on the Kansas prairie are handled with

realism and dense fact. One can sense the prairie wind, smell the sod houses, hear the sound of wheels and hooves in the muddy streets. The sound of frontier speech, with its combined influences of Southern, rural, city slicker, and English immigrant strains is well rendered. The style is undecorated and direct, with none of the poetic lilt of *The Good Earth,* that story of another stay-at-home.

While there was some disagreement among critics concerning the artistic merits and importance of the John Sedges novels, there never existed any question in anyone's mind but that here was an American writer with a broad appeal to American readers. By the time the fifth of the series was published, it had become common knowledge that John Sedges was Pearl Buck; the point was proved, and the pseudonym abandoned. All this time Pearl was also writing and publishing other books under her own name.

In *The Townsman,* as well as in the other books of the John Sedges group, runs the theme of the responsible citizen, the conflict between duty and impulse. This question arose many times in Pearl's life and work. When it is depicted as a problem besetting talented and sensitive women, as in so many of her books, the reader may be aware that the author is dipping deeply into her own life for her material.

Many times in her books there occurs the strong woman, gifted in a variety of skills, who accepts responsibility for helping and supporting her parents and children, usually at some sacrifice of her own desires. She wants all of life—family, home, love, career—but finds these things in conflict. The men in her life are usually inadequate and unequal to her in intellect or moral strength. Each of these women is wrapped in loneliness. Perhaps "alone" is a better word than "lonely."

So it is with Susan Gaylord, the heroine of *This Proud Heart*. It is particularly revealing about men, women, and Pearl Buck that when Blake Kinnaird comes for a final farewell to Susan, he tells her, "You're only half there. A man likes to possess his wife."

So it is, too, with Joan Richards, the heroine of *The Time Is Noon,* a novel written in the 30's but not published until 1967. Joan becomes the pillar of strength when her mother dies, taking upon herself the task of mothering her sister and brother and assisting her father, a minister, in his work. When the family breaks up—her father dies, the sister marries a missionary to China, and the brother goes off to become an aviator—her life is empty. Aching for children, she marries a handsome but coarse farmer with an even coarser and more unfeeling family, and quickly realizes she has made a mistake. But, loyal and responsible, she hangs on. Her first child is retarded, but after her sister and brother-in-law are killed in a Chinese uprising, she adopts their children, who have been rescued. She divorces her husband finally, and against great odds sets up on her own in the little town she has always lived in. The second man in her life, whom she truly loves, is already married and morally bound to his frail, sick wife. But Joan will take whatever love comes her way from this relationship. She does not need marriage, for she has the children to love and care for, and she is secure in her own independence. For a moment she wishes that she, too, were frail and protected by someone stronger, but that is not to be, for she will always be the stronger. And for her there are the satisfactions of the strong—devotion to weaker ones and proud aloneness.

In another book, *Pavilion of Women,* the theme of a strong woman's independence, relations with men, and assumption of responsibility is further explored, this time in a Chinese setting.

The heroine is Madame Wu, brilliant, searching, aristocratic. On reaching her fortieth birthday she decides that she will no longer serve the physical needs of her husband, which are distasteful to her, although she has been a model wife up to then. Her husband is a kind but foolish man and not nearly her equal in mind or sensitivity. Strong, able, and clever, she manages all the affairs of the household and farms. Everyone —sons, daughters-in-law, servants, neighbors—turns to her for leadership. She is skilled in manipulating people to do what she thinks best while making them believe it is their own desire. Most of this skill is now turned to relieving herself of such responsibilities, so that she can at last do what she has always wanted to do—cultivate her probing mind and seek knowledge.

She meets a priest, a brilliant and saintly man called Brother André, who has given up all material pleasures and needs for a life of service to humanity. They have long philosophical talks, and through him Madame Wu feels her mind and heart expand toward a world view. And for the first time she knows a man who is her mental equal or superior, and one even stronger and more independent than she. He makes her see that all her manipulation of others has been for selfish reasons and that she has treated people as objects and pieces of property.

After André is killed by robbers, Madame Wu realizes that she loved him and that she has never truly loved anyone else. She then devotes herself to less selfish pursuits, arranging the affairs of her children to suit their needs rather than hers, and she continues André's philanthropic work in the village.

She is still strong, responsible, supremely alone—but now she serves, instead of uses, people.

One cannot help but feel that there is much of Pearl Buck in Madame Wu—the overpowering sense of being alone and unable to share completely, the appearance of strength, the conflicting inner need to find someone stronger and smarter, the ability to manipulate people and events, the boundless sense of responsibility, the occasional wild desire to shuck off every burden and be utterly free.

Here, too, we find another theme running strongly—the yearning for spiritual belief even after religious faith has gone. At the end of the book, when Madame Wu realizes how deeply she had loved André and how fulfilling his work of love had been, the author writes:

> Yes, she now believed that when her body died, her soul would go on. Gods she did not worship, and faith she had none, but love she had and forever. Love alone had awakened her sleeping soul and had made it deathless.
>
> She knew she was immortal.

Again and again the idea came up in her books. There must be a life of the spirit, she felt. Surely something flowed through human beings, something more than just the sum of blood and flesh and nerves, that did not end when death closed one's eyes and shriveled the cells. Some readers would scoff at this and call it sentimentality, and it would frequently provide the point where she and Richard Walsh would part thinking company, but the sense of it remained strong in her. Even *Mandala,* a love story set in India, published in 1970, ends with the suggestion that the spirit of a prince's son killed in battle has been reincarnated in a child. Interestingly, it is an American woman, in love with the father, who first believes the event and shows evidence of it to the doubting prince who has turned away from the ancient beliefs of his people.

The heroine of this book is yet another version of the alone, independent, accomplished woman seeking to find a union of mind, body, and spirit. She might well be Pearl Buck's own young delegate—in fact, the heroine is carrying on a life style suggested to her by her grandmother (who resembles Pearl Buck in many ways) and which is best expressed as the injunction to live as freely and independently as one can: "Avoid antipathies, follow your sympathies!"

With the themes so far noted there is also mingled a vast concern for what was happening in the world and the conviction that the only way to deal with the world's troubles is through better understanding between nations and races, love for humankind, and unrelenting struggle against those who would destroy freedom.

Throughout World War II Pearl Buck wrote novels—*Dragon Seed* and *The Promise* are examples—that dramatized what was happening in Asia at that time. They told the story of the fighting in China and Burma and Japan, and predicted that the end of the war would see the downfall of white power over colored peoples.

When the war was over she wrote *Command the Morning,* a novel about the development of the atom bomb. In it she traces the doubts of the scientists about the morality of using such an awesome weapon on people. The men scientists in the book are led by patriotism and "realism" to complete their work and stand by while the bomb is dropped. But the women of the book, including a woman scientist, are horrified by the act and will not cooperate in a project so immoral and destructive of life. The book contains the warning that women are not heard in the councils of the world, and that this must and will change.

In *Command the Morning* there is the bitter comment that the first use of the atom bomb was by a white nation against a brown one, and it warns that the dark-skinned portion of the world—its largest—will remember that.

Not only in novels, but in articles and speeches she hammered away at the idea that the people of the world are one family. There will be no peace until there is equality and understanding among nations.

The plight of the black people in America, the treatment of orphans, the problems of retarded children, the role of women in society—all these were subjects for stories, essays and articles. Pearl Buck had much to say, warnings to make, lessons to teach, causes to uphold; she would not be silenced, and she did not hesitate to use her craft for such ends.

That was what gave her critics trouble. They charged that much of her writing was openly propagandistic. They said that the artistic quality of her work suffered as a result. In order to make her points, she manipulated her characters too obviously, sometimes having them do illogical things that did not spring from their character or from the natural drive of the story. People and events in a novel, especially in the realistic type of novel that Pearl Buck wrote, must above all be believable, but her events sometimes strained the reader's belief and her characters sometimes moved like puppets, said her more sophisticated readers.

They also said that in the sheer quantity of her output, her writing style had become unexciting and ordinary, imitative of popular magazine fashions, and out of touch with the truly important developments in literature. If this was what she wanted, said those who surveyed the literary scene, either because she needed the money or because she simply needed to write in such vast quantity, that was perfectly all right, but the writer who had written the Nobel Prize masterpieces could no longer be seriously discussed as a major American writer. Following World War II, most of her books were never even reviewed by the critics.

Most probably this hurt her. But it did not change her. She had made her decisions long ago, and she knew who she was and what she would do.

She would "follow her sympathies" and let happen what would.

Fifteen

"Take Your Own Cause!"

The critics saw it as a failing that so many of Pearl Buck's novels were marked by "didacticism," meaning that these novels were too much influenced by her social messages. Pearl would surely agree that her novels encased her views about life and the world's affairs. Stories should have meaning, she felt, and the meaning should be made clear. And she had many things to say.

The concerned writer, she thought, needed to think about his responsibilities as a citizen, and if he were to be a total person, he could not split himself into his "artistic" life and his political life. Worse, he should not try to live only as an artist and abandon his responsibilities as a citizen. To care only for art and not for the world made only half a person and diminished the artist's usefulness.

Pearl's own causes not only furnished meaning for her books but also for much of that part of her life she spent away from her desk. They led her onto the lecture platform, into the writing of "propaganda" material, and into the affairs of various organizations. She did not like that part of it, for she was naturally shy. Public speaking was painful to her. Committee meetings were often boring to the point of pain. But however much she wanted to be a private person, her fame had made a public person of her, and her opinions and activity were sought. Even if they were not sought, she would have volunteered them, because it seemed hollow to her to write about freedom at her desk and then turn away the needful stranger at the door. One had to act, not merely write, one's beliefs. If a thing needed to be done, why then, do it and do not wait.

To a young woman who once complained wearily that political leaders offered no causes worth fighting for, Pearl burst out impatiently, "Oh, take your own cause!" Absalom and Caroline Sydenstricker's daughter had inherited more of the missionary spirit than she knew.

Surely no thinking person could stay aloof from the war against Germany and Japan. Pearl had for a long time predicted such a struggle and she was glad that the democratic countries had at last taken up arms against fascism and repression. But she knew, and had so written, that many of these democratic countries were themselves guilty of repressive policies against the Asian and African colonies they dominated and against racial or religious minorities at home. The upheaval caused by the war would sharpen the hunger for freedom in these colonies and minorities—and the world would never be the same again. The war presented an opportunity for freedom not only for the victims of German and Japanese imperialism but for the oppressed in the empires of all nations, including those who now found themselves among the Allies. It had come as she had expected.

"I am not disturbed by war," Pearl told a writer for the *Saturday Review of Literature*. "I've never lived in certainty. I follow the Chinese theme—to keep the changeless self in the midst of ten thousand changes."

For her own country she saw a special role in this world-wide conflict. Even though America's record was tarnished by racial prejudice at home, it enjoyed a heritage of freedom; its democracy was admired; and it was relatively free of the kind of colonialism for which other Allies, like England, France, and the Netherlands, were so hated in Asia and Africa. The United States, she felt, could now play a unique role in helping new nations find democratic and independent ways of life. As part of such leadership, the United States would have to prove its sincerity by cleaning up intolerance and racial inequality at home, particularly against its black citizens.

She told the same reporter, "if we intend to persist blindly in our racial prejudice, then we are fighting on the wrong side in this war. We belong with Hitler. For the white man can no longer rule in this world unless he rules by totalitarian military force."

Besides seeking every means of keeping such aims before the public, one of the most useful things she felt she was qualified to do was to explain Asia to Americans and America to Asians. Thus she could help pave the way for the friendship and cooperation needed not only in winning the war but in expanding the peace.

It was to this purpose that, in the early years of the war, she took over the direction of *Asia Magazine* and also founded the East and West Association. Throughout the war the East and West Association brought to the United States lecturers and performers from China, Indochina, and India, and arranged for them to tour clubs and schools. Many thousands of Americans were thus introduced to Chinese and Indian acting troupes and dancers, and from Eastern scholars they could hear at first-hand about the rich traditions of these ancient civilizations.

The medium of radio offered a way to reach many more millions of people, and Pearl was determined to use it. Quietly and anonymously, she attended classes in radio writing techniques and, so prepared, she wrote a number of radio programs in support of the war, some to be used by United China Relief. She wrote seven radio dramas in Mandarin Chinese for the government to broadcast to the Orient, explaining the American way of life and the war aims as she saw them.

But she did not give blind support to the war or to the country. Pearl was enough aware of the ways of nations and politicians to realize that there were many in the United States who saw the war not as a chance for world freedom but as an opportunity to replace European colonial power with American might. And it gave her anguish that prejudice against black citizens continued.

In an article in *Asia Magazine* she pointed out how this affected the war in Asia. We could not win the war or arrange a lasting peace in Asia unless we found unity of purpose with the Chinese people, she said, "But of course there is no use going to the Chinese if in the state of mind behind this union there is a race prejudice or if there are feelings of national or cultural superiority. The Chinese will discover such a state of mind at once, and it will not be possible for them to unite with us."

In a letter to *The New York Times* in 1942 she blasted racial prejudice in the Armed Forces, in labor unions, and in defense industries. She warned the nation that tragedy would result from the despair and anger of its black community.

"Young colored men and women today are giving up hope for justice or security in their own country," she wrote. "When this hopelessness reaches down to certain strata in any society, outbreaks of crime are inevitable. We must expect it in many places besides Harlem." End prejudice now, she pleaded to the American people, "don't accept the stupidities of race prejudice." She linked this issue to the war: "Everywhere in the world colored people are asking each other if they must forever endure the arrogant ruling white class. They feel they have been very long patient, but they cannot be patient forever, and they will not."

She was sensitive to this mood of despair among American Negroes and she knew that because of it black Americans were not actively supporting the war. She understood and sympathized with this, writing again in *Asia Magazine* that many Negroes were so dissatisfied with American conditions that they actually hoped for a Japanese victory, feeling that anything would be better than white rule.

She understood that mood, but she felt it was wrong, and so she wrote a letter to all Negro newspapers in which she pointed out that Japan, like Hitler's Germany, was founded on the subjugation of the individual. Although America was torn over racial prejudice, she wrote, its foundations were in individual liberty, and in this war America stood for freedom. She pleaded with the black community to help America find and know itself. While Negroes should always remember their wrongs, they should not seek vengeance but instead support the idea of freedom in this war and so provide an example of courage and generosity.

"I know this is no small thing to ask of any people. Certainly it is asking you to be better than the white man has been.

But indeed you must be better than the white man has been. For if those who have suffered learn nothing from their suffering, then the world is lost indeed. Who can fight so well for freedom as those who know what it is to be deprived of it?"

She emphasized this message to young black Americans in June of 1942 when, as a trustee of Howard University, a black college, she spoke at the commencement ceremony. She cited the prejudice that faced these young people and how it would seem easier to avoid that prejudice by remaining isolated in the black community: ". . . you can consider that it will be safest for you to stay inside your own nation, the Negro nation of a white America that will gradually cease to develop in its growth toward a true democracy because of its own division. Or you can determine that you are going to help America be that true democracy of which we all dream."

The fight for racial equality, she told the graduates, was not a war between races or between East and West. "Your enemies are not of one race or nation, your enemies are all those who do not believe in human equality. . . . You too must not yield to race prejudice. It is as wrong for you to hate the white man because he is white as it is for him to hate you because you are not white."

She urged, "Come out of that little world of your own and take your place in America as interpreters of the colored peoples of the world. Be ready to speak for Africa at the peace table, and to speak for Korea. Make yourselves the part of America to whom these peoples turn for understanding. Today you belong in the world, and your demands in our country are part of the world demand for freedom and for human equality."

But even in the year she made that speech she could see that in the way the war was being waged there was yet no clear commitment among the Allies to end discrimination and colonial rule. Indeed, with new military victories, it seemed that the Allies no longer felt the need even to give much lip service to such aims. Angrily Pearl told a dinner gathering of Nobel Prize winners: "None of us here is safe. Our kind anywhere is not safe. All the victories now being won do not make us safe. Those of us who are Jews are not safe, here or anywhere else in the world. Those of us who are women are not safe here or anywhere else in the world. The determination to continue rule over colonial empires endangers us, the vowed will to maintain white supremacy at all costs in our own country endangers us. All those who belong to those testing places of democracy, the minorities, the Jews, the Negroes, the women, are endangered. All who are the agents of civilization, the intellectuals, the poets and artists and writers, the liberal in mind, the thinkers, the men and women of ideas, the idealists, are endangered."

Anger and disappointment were to stay with her after the war ended. Even in 1946, at the founding of the United Nations, she could see no basis for hoping that the United States would help bring freedom to colonial lands. Indeed, in Indochina the United States was helping France reestablish power over French colonies there. She was dismayed, for she knew that there would be certain revolution against outside rule in such countries as Korea and Vietnam and that the American involvement there would lead to certain tragedy for the United States and earn the bitter hatred of Asian people.

As for China she felt that American policy was a disaster. The Chinese Communists had proved to be the strongest force in China, and Chiang Kai-shek had been forced to flee with his Nationalist army to the offshore island of Taiwan. The United

States continued to support Chiang Kai-shek and protected him in his island with warships, refusing to recognize Communist China. Pearl felt it was a sad mistake. She was not an admirer of Communism, and she often spoke out against its repression of individual liberty and its harsh treatment of dissenters. Nevertheless, this was now the government of the most populous nation on earth, and it had to be included in the family of nations. If the United States had been friendly to it, we would have been able to stay in touch and perhaps encourage the less stern and harsh elements among the Chinese Communists. In such conflicts, certain to arise in other Asian nations in the years to come, America should be neutral and take no sides, she felt.

She knew that Communism was not the same in all countries and that Communists differed among themselves just as capitalists did. Blind refusal to deal with Communist governments was stupid, she felt, and small-minded. But in the years after World War II, fear of Communism gripped many American political leaders, and liberals who spoke of such things as brotherhood among nations, political tolerance, and racial equality were themselves suspected of being Communists. In such an atmosphere *Asia Magazine* and the East and West Association found it increasingly difficult to operate. Sadly Pearl closed them both. To help fight against this new tide of intolerance, which now threatened the right of Americans to criticize their government openly, she joined and served on the national committee of the American Civil Liberties Union, an organization providing legal help to persons persecuted for their beliefs.

With sinking heart, she saw in the anti-Communist panic the end of the hope that a reasonable way to end war would be found. In 1949, with other writers, scientists, educators, and labor leaders, she participated as a sponsor of a pamphlet warning that the United States was heading for militarism. The pamphlet detailed the rising budget for armies and bombs, the continuation of the draft, the increasing number of military men who had influence in government, foreign policy, and education, and the close links between the military and industrial leaders. This was not the role Pearl had hoped America would play.

Almost a decade later, in 1958, she was still sadly criticizing American policy. In *Friend to Friend,* an exchange of views with the Philippine leader Carlos P. Romulo, she noted bitterly that the United States, after having led the way by granting independence to the Philippines, then gave its support to the old colonial powers in Indochina. American policy had compelled the Chinese and Vietnamese Communists to rely entirely on Russia when they might have looked to the United States for support and friendly relations. Instead of understanding and seeking the friendship of rising national movements in Asia, "we have chosen to build a chain of military bases in the Aleutians, Japan, Okinawa, Korea, Guam, Formosa, the Philippines, a semicircle useless if the peoples it contains are against us.

"Can we be surprised if we are mocked," she wrote, "as we deserve to be when we declare all men free and equal and then deny the affirmation every day of our lives in the way we behave toward our own minorities? And when we have behaved in like manner to the Asians, and do so behave, limiting our annual immigration quota to a hundred each from the oldest and wisest nations on the globe, can we be surprised that those nations doubt the validity of our ideals?"

That very year black children, following the Supreme Court decision to end segregation in education, had been blocked at the school doors by screaming, stone-throwing mobs of whites. Pearl wrote, "Asian eyes look upon Americans stoning our own Negro citizens, they see American faces distorted by hatred against dark-skinned people like themselves.

"I have before me the pictures of some of the people in Little Rock, Arkansas. These pictures have been flashed around the world and it is true they have done our nation incalculable harm. I have studied them well. They are bewildered faces of discontented adolescents, ignorant men, angry women. It grieves me to think that millions of people who have no opportunity to see the many good American faces, so many more than these few, will look at these with terror and astonishment and say to themselves and to each other, 'So this is the way Americans look!'"

How, she wrote to Carlos Romulo, would it be possible to show the world the real America, its honesty of public argument and self-criticism, its sense of humor, its basic democratic ideals?

Another cause that occupied Pearl Buck's attention was the liberation of women. Her novels dealt in many ways with the special problems of women. In her own life, of course, she had carved out an independent and free way of life for herself and in the process she had not surrendered a particle of her femininity. That not all women could achieve such independence, she was well aware, but she felt that the fault was not only in the ways of the world or in the oppression by men; women themselves shared responsibility for their dependent status.

"The truth," she wrote in *Of Men and Women,* "is that

women in America too easily accept the idea of their inferiority to men—if not actually, then in order to curry favor with men, who imagine it easier to live with inferiors than with equals."

It was necessary for women to insist on self-fulfillment. "For if the intelligent woman obeys the voice of tradition and limits herself to the traditional four walls, she joins the vast ranks of the nervous, restless, average American woman whose whimsies torture her family, who spoils the good name of all women because she is often flighty, unreliable, without good judgment in affairs, and given to self-pity."

It was a profound problem for men, too. "When will American men learn that they cannot expect happiness with a wife who is not allowed to develop her whole self? A restless, unfulfilled woman is not going to be a satisfied wife or a satisfactory lover. It is not that 'women are like that.' Anyone would be 'like that' if he were put into such circumstances— that is, trained and developed for opportunities later denied."

But could not many men also complain that they, too, were denied opportunity? "Yes, but the times have done it and not tradition. There is a difference. And one man has as good a chance as another to win or lose, even in hard times. But no woman has even a man's chance in hard times, or in any times."

For a woman to fulfill herself she did not have to imitate a man, Pearl insisted. "The truth is that if a woman is a real woman and proud to be one, nothing can quench the essential femininity of her being. She may sit on a throne and rule a nation, she may sit upon a bench and be a judge, she may be the foreman in a mill, she could if she would be a bridge builder or a machinist or anything else; and if she were proud of herself as a woman her work would be well done and her femininity deepened. It is when women undervalue themselves as women that they ape men and become mannish and arouse dislike in all their fellows, men and women. No kind of work can spoil the quality of a woman unless she has first spoiled it herself by wishing consciously or unconsciously that she were not a woman."

It was an essential part of Pearl Buck's own quality as a woman that she devoted herself to the cause of children. She could not resist a child, especially the child handicapped by birth or circumstance. Her own, and only, natural child had been retarded, and the care of this child remained a deep personal concern throughout her life. The concern spread to all retarded children, whose problems she studied and whose welfare she promoted. Her book *The Child Who Never Grew* dramatized this problem and helped many others to face it. She busied herself in the affairs of the Association of Parents of the Mentally Retarded, helping to bring to light the problem of care for such children. She was active on the board of directors of the institution where her own retarded child stayed.

Her knowledge of the subject and her willingness to act caused the governor of Pennsylvania to appoint her chairman of the Governor's Committee for the Handicapped, and she used this office to bring about greater unity and cooperation among the many competing agencies in the field. Despite her dislike of meetings and speeches, she proved to be a strong and effective organizer.

The problems of orphans were especially close to her, for her own family consisted of adopted children. She had been in many orphan homes and adoption agencies. What she saw and experienced there appalled her. She felt that many children in these places were prevented from being adopted by cold, bureaucratic, and arbitrary rules and frequently by racial, religious, and social snobbery. Some institutions, she found to her shock, deliberately discouraged adoption in order to keep their number of orphaned charges high and thus acquire funds. She publicized these matters whenever she could, discussed them with social workers and officials.

In 1947 a special problem in orphans came to her attention. An adoption agency called her; they had a half-white, half-East Indian baby born to an American missionary's daughter. There had been no marriage, and the family had refused to accept the little boy. The agency could find no proper parents, for it was the custom to "match" adopted children to the racial characteristics of the adoptive parents. Pearl was outraged by this notion of matching. "Send him to me!" she stated immediately.

Almost at the same time another baby boy, the child of a Chinese surgeon and an American nurse, was also brought into her family because no matching parents could be found.

Furious at this situation, and realizing that many such interracial orphans existed, she and Richard Walsh gathered together a group of neighbors, among whom was the song writer Oscar Hammerstein, and together they formed their own adoption agency. Called "Welcome House," it sought to find adoptive homes in the community for children of mixed parentage. The only "match" was that of love, and Pearl found this in abundance among the people who lived in Bucks County.

If such biracial children were a problem in the United States, they presented even more serious a problem in Asia. Traveling through Japan and Korea, she was made aware of large numbers of Amerasian—half American, half Asian— children. Wherever American soldiers and sailors had been, such children soon began to be born. About one out of every ten American servicemen in Asia left behind a fatherless child. The Asian mothers of these children generally were ashamed of them, and the families felt disgraced. The children were neglected at home and scorned by other children. In Korea Pearl saw them begging on the streets.

Even when these children were loved and cared for by their mothers, at school they were tormented and insulted by teachers and classmates. When they grew up they could not find jobs, and so they roamed the streets, bitter outcasts. Their faces haunted Pearl, and she grieved at such waste.

The problem went beyond the unhappiness and stunted lives of these Amerasian waifs. "I believe," she wrote, "that these children, cared for and educated, can be a blessing to the countries where they are born. I know that, uncared for and allowed to grow up in ignorance, they can be a source of trouble which will react upon us all. We know well what neglected children can do in our own country. But these are internationally neglected children, and there will be international repercussions."

Who would accept responsibility? Pearl went to government officials. While they recognized the problem, they could do nothing, for it was official policy to ignore the existence of these children. She called the veterans' organizations, hoping to interest them in the problem, for after all, these were the children of American servicemen. But there was no response.

Very well, then, she would do it herself. To bring these children for adoption to America did not really solve the problem. For one, only a limited number of American families would accept them. Most of the children were not available for adoption—they *had* mothers—and large numbers were enough grown up to consider themselves not Americans but Koreans, Japanese, or—in more recent years—Vietnamese. The challenge was to find ways of giving them a better chance for usefulness and happiness in the land of their birth.

This meant help in all ways—clothes, schools, and careers. An agency needed to be created that would serve as father to these fatherless boys and girls. Some who qualified could be brought to the United States for training as professionals and returned home with useful skills. At the same time Asian employers and government agencies had to be persuaded to hire such reclaimed outcasts and see them for the valuable citizens they were.

To these ends Pearl established the Pearl S. Buck Foundation, and to it she signed away most of her considerable fortune —savings, real-estate holdings, royalties from books and movies. The earnings of most of her new books and articles were earmarked for the foundation. She found a director, hired a staff, and the work was on its way. About a hundred people are employed by the foundation, and most of them are to be found in office and field in Korea, Taiwan, Thailand, the Philippines, Japan, and Vietnam—wherever in Asia American soldiers are stationed—searching for and helping Amerasian children.

For Pearl there always was a clear connection between seeing need, acting, accepting responsibility. It was this attitude that from 1958 to 1966 led her to accept the post of president of the Writers' Guild. Those who worked with her in that organization remember that her presence at any meeting seemed to have the effect of quieting voices and smoothing tempers, even though this was a period in which the guild was going through major changes. Her impatience with details and her sense of direction kept sessions moving when she chaired them.

In much the same way, when she began spending her summers in Vermont, she set about the task of reviving the once-lovely little town of Danby, which was dying because its industry had gone and its young people were going. She bought real estate along the Main Street, found tenants who would restore the homes and shops to their former charm, formed a town construction and decorating company staffed by young people, and organized activities that would bring tourists and more business to the area.

This was basically a simple idea, and the simple approach was one Pearl admired. She said of her friend Eleanor Roosevelt, with whom she worked in many of her causes, "She was so absolutely honest! I think we Americans, being so young and unsophisticated, have a completely wrong idea of what true sophistication is. According to Asian definition, which I myself believe to be correct, a sophisticated person is one who has experienced everything, knows everything, and has reduced everything to its essence. Sophistication is the final simplicity. And of course that was Mrs. Roosevelt."

And Pearl Buck, too.

Sixteen

❧

Meet Pearl Buck

In a sycamore-lined block in Philadelphia stands a stately town house with an inviting, graceful door. It is the American headquarters of the Pearl S. Buck Foundation.

It was to the Philadelphia headquarters of the foundation that the biographer came to speak with Pearl Buck, for he planned to tell the story of her life. A secretary, a soft-spoken woman, welcomed him in. Immediately past the entrance the visitor was in the special world of Pearl Buck, whose Asian touch and taste commands this place. The feeling of Asia is not only in the Chinese artifacts—vases, screens, furniture, chests—for the visitor would sense it even if the furniture were of another style. Asia is in the balance and order of every item in these rooms, the cool glowing surfaces, the harmony and blend of color, the spot of orange tinged with rust, the rich browns, the delicate lemons.

The elevator hummed the biographer to the top floor, and a quiet young man led him to the author's study, where he was to wait. Calm and harmony ruled this book-lined room. To one side was the great desk, its square surface gleaming, solid as rock, and the visitor knew it instantly as the very same from which Pearl Buck, writing *The Good Earth,* could see Nanking's Purple Mountain. From it one now could see the sun-dappled trees outside. A pair of easy chairs covered in a strong light-colored fabric, with a table between, waited for the conversation, and here the writer sat only a few moments before the great white door opened again and Pearl Buck came in and he was on his feet, holding her hand.

The astonishing eyes first, Arctic blue-white, remote, bottomless, extraordinarily alert, missing nothing, delicate yet powerful as great sapphires in their etch of mascara. Then one was aware of the fine, clear, fresh skin and the pile of silver hair, so vivid against the deep blue suit. With some surprise one noted how large she was and yet how lightly she moved.

She answered questions directly in a small voice, cool and musical. The enunciation was precise, in accent of no region at all except for a certain lingering on the s-s-s-s and sh-h-h-h-h.

We talked of childhood and the business of growing up.

I wasn't a communicative child at all. I never shared my thinking with anybody. The truth is, I don't think I ever shared anything of my inner self with anyone. Indeed, I still can't bear to have anyone ask me, "What are you writing now?" If you tell the story you're working on, the life goes out of it.

My parents, though, let me be. I was an extraordinarily free child and I lived my own life. And I have tried to let my own children grow in their own ways. I do not discipline them or try to change them. If they want to do things because that is the way I do them, that is fine. If not, then not. I have respect for their personalities. They are all individualists because they have been allowed to develop that way. People tell me my children were spoiled. Perhaps. But most mothers, I observe, hover a good deal over their children. I never hover, I don't feel I have a right to interfere with a child's personality.

Of her brother and sister. When she bought the farmhouse in Pennsylvania, her older brother Edwin bought a house nearby across the stream and nearly within hailing distance. He was never to live in it, though, for he died of a heart attack when it was ready. Grace went to live in Washington, D.C., married a fine man, and became the mother of three brilliant children. Under the pen name Cornelia Spencer she wrote several children's books, one of which was a biography of her famous sister. But Pearl was not fond of that biography, for it was too uncritical, she felt.

She is an affectionate, warm, and generous person and confides in me still, although I do not confide in anyone. She will always be, I suppose, my little sister.

We talked of marriage and of men and women.

I have had doubts whether a woman like me should ever marry, in justice to the man. I can be remote. In both my marriages I had the feeling I was hardly fair to the man.

John Buck was a good man. I used to feel sorry for him because he deserved a good wife. It wasn't his fault that we were so different. He married a very suitable Chinese woman, his secretary, who made him that good wife, and has had two nice children. After my second husband's death, John wrote me a sympathetic letter and his wife did, too—a "younger sisterly" letter—inviting me to come to see them, but I had no wish to go, even though I pass their home quite close on my way to my summer house in Vermont.

In 1953 Richard Walsh suffered a stroke that severely damaged his brain. For the next seven years he lived thus, his speech and perception and ability to respond fading away. In their life together they had never spent a night apart and it continued that way through most of the years he took in dying. She read books to him when his eyes failed and played music for him until the day came when even that ceased to have meaning for him and she knew she had to pick up the threads of her own life. She left for a trip to Japan in order to work with a film production of her children's book, *The Big Wave,* and while she was there he passed away quietly. It had been a long good-bye, and she was ready for it. Shortly afterward, she wrote a book about that time, *A Bridge for Passing.* "It is not true that one never walks alone," she wrote. "There is an eternity where one walks alone and we do not know its end."

But always there would be work, empty pages lying on the desk waiting to be filled in. She was sixty-eight when Richard died and there was still much to be done. There was time to heal and in that time the past twenty-five years, too, would be put in their place.

And she could gaze past the biographer to the window, where the sun touched the sycamore leaves and made them glow as if from within, and say, half dreaming,

My second husband—my "real" husband—was a charming companion and wonderful to live with. But he had no sense of wonder. He could not stand speculative thinking. What has kept me the happiest has been the wonder. I have always had a sense of it, and there is as much to wonder about today as when I was a child. Life is full of it. Even this moment there is wonder in the sun on those leaves.

After Richard Walsh died, hundreds of sympathetic letters were sent to her from people, great and small, she had met all over the world. One of the warmest and most touching of these came from Ernest Hocking. The retired chairman of

Harvard's philosophy department had met Pearl in China about thirty years before and had met her again when she had defended his report on the missionary movement. Throughout the years he had watched her career, had periodically corresponded with her, and occasionally they had met and talked.

With the letter he sent a copy of his book *The Meaning of Immortality,* which he had written after his wife died some ten years before. The book examined the question of the continuation of the spirit, pondered about the soul, and suggested the philosophy that if something ought to be, it will be. He begged Pearl to visit him at his retirement house in New Hampshire.

The letter and the book touched her deeply. She had wondered about such questions, always had and always would, and she did not feel, although she was nonreligious, that nonbelievers had any answers for them.

She had come to spend the summers in Danby, Vermont, where she had built a house to escape the ragweed of Pennsylvania. That August she drove over to New Hampshire and visited Ernest Hocking. He was eighty-eight years old then, twenty years older than she, but still amazingly vigorous, with clear eyes, a ruddy face, strong white hair, and clipped moustache. "I remember the feeling of recognition that passed between us." There are moments when people are ready for each other.

"The heart, it seems, can never know its age."

They talked. They walked. They rowed a boat across the lake. Their minds probed, reached for meaning in all the wonders between men and women, the thrust of science, the persistence of mystery and faith. It seemed their minds had always been companions. His intelligence, at eighty-eight, was still fresh and energetic, and the quality of his thinking exhilarated her. He loved to speculate, to think of what might be, to wonder what wisdom lay beyond knowledge.

In the evenings they sat before the great fireplace and, holding hands, watched the last light of dusk on the White Mountains peaks that could be seen through the window.

Ernest did enter into philosophy with all the power of his fine brain. Yes, there was an affinity, there was no doubt. But I did not want to marry him. I didn't want to live there. I didn't want to marry anymore. That was finished.

For the next five years, until he died, she saved a portion of late summer for him, going to stay with him at his home, alone except for the old housekeeper. He had a fine library, and it was a good place to work. During the rest of the year they exchanged affectionate letters and poems.

That was a wonderful experience. I think I supplied for him in those last lonely years the sort of affection and personal relationship that helped him over the end. For me, I took such great pleasure in his remarkably clear mind. I gave him love, but I don't want that misunderstood. It was the love of a human being for another human being. It was respect and admiration and a deep sense of attachment to a really noble person, a friendship of like mind. And it was such a joy because his mind was really better than mine, and I had never had that experience before.

He knew when he was nearing death, and he sent her a usual affectionate note that concluded with the Latin words, *Morituri te salutamus* ("We who are about to die salute you"). But she did not go to him when he lay dying. He belonged then to his children, she thought, and she did not want to remember him in decline, as she remembered Richard Walsh.

And so he died. And she was so experienced now in the ways of sorrow. And she knew herself.

All my close friends are men. I don't think I have any intimate woman friends. My life has been more with men than with women. And the men, those I married and those I knew, taken together have given me a rich life. Each has given me something. If you ask me has there been any one man who filled my life—no! My first marriage gave me a home, somebody who cared about my existence and to whom I had a responsibility. My second marriage, a lovely day-to-day companionship in all things but the philosophical. Ernest Hocking gave me what neither of the others did. And I have had men friends—each in his own way. Nobody finds everything in one person.

And she would go on. She would travel, speaking for the Amerasian children. The mail would bring letters from all over the world, from readers and friends both humble and distinguished—housewives, mechanics, diplomats, princes. And the fine, firm hand, the one the biographer held again a moment in farewell, would go on scratching away for a portion of each day, filling sheets of paper, stacking them high. For there were books yet to write and she had to hurry to get them down while she could. And now and then the pen would stop, and she would look up at the sycamore leaves, or at the Green Mountains of Vermont, or out the window of a jetliner—and she would wonder about life's mystery as she had wondered all her life. Sometimes the wondering would be a nourishment for the tiring spirit, or sometimes a way to fill an empty hour, but more often it would be a hurt, a void that wanted to be filled.

For life is basically sad. We are poised here for a little while, and we can enjoy this through our minds and our senses, but we don't know anything, really. To my mind this is the utmost cruelty, that creatures are created who know that they don't know anything and can't know anything about themselves—where they came from and where they are going. And therefore we must say that life is sad, and I have always, even as a child burying the remains of little babies beyond the city wall, accepted that fact.

And the moments of happiness are in small things, if you are in tune to them.

Not long after this interview, Pearl Buck entered a year of increasing ill health, involving several stays in the hospital and surgery. She died on March 6, 1973, at her home in Danby, Vermont, and she worked almost every day to the end.

SELECTED READING

The list of all of Pearl S. Buck's writings is too long and it might dismay the young reader; besides, any library can provide it. The author recommends to those who wish an introduction to Pearl Buck to begin with *The Good Earth.* For more of her novels about China, *The Mother, Sons,* and *Pavilion of Women* make good reading.

The best of her "John Sedges" novels is *The Townsmen. This Proud Heart, The Time Is Noon,* and *Command the Morning* are representative of her novels on American themes. *Mandala,* a tale set in India, was published in 1970. *The Story Bible* and a picture book, *China Past and Present,* appeared in 1972.

She is, of course, the best authority on her own life, and young readers should enjoy her autobiographical *My Several Worlds* and *A Bridge for Passing.* Her biographies of her mother and her father, *The Exile* and *Fighting Angel,* are superb portraits and compelling to read.

Index

About the Author

Irvin Block was born in Pittsburgh and grew up in Cleveland. At Western Reserve University, where he took every course offered in English, writing, and drama, he graduated with honors. After his service in World War II, he bought a typewriter and moved to New York to begin his career as a writer. Since that time he has written everything from adventure stories to technical articles on medical research, as well as a number of books for young readers.

With his wife and children, Mr. Block now lives in Sea Cliff, New York. Next to family and writing he loves sailing best—the Blocks have cruised all along the New England-Long Island Sound shore in their sloop. For all his achievements, Mr. Block describes himself as "a moderately accomplished photographer, an indifferent but earnest classical guitarist, and a gifted idler."

MAY 12 '75

602/178